GINO'S
PASTA

This book is dedicated to all my fans who have been there for me from the beginning, you are truly *fantastico!*

Gino D'Acampo

GINO'S PASTA

EVERYTHING YOU NEED TO COOK THE ITALIAN WAY

Photography by Kate Whitaker

KYLE BOOKS

This edition printed in Great Britain in 2011 by
Kyle Books
23 Howland Street
London W1T 4AY
general.enquiries@kylebooks.com
www.kylebooks.com

First published in 2010 by Kyle Cathie Limited

ISBN 978 1 85626 975 9

A Cataloguing in Publication record for this title is
available from the British Library.

10 9 8 7 6 5 4 3

Gino D'Acampo is hereby identified as the author of this
work in accordance with Section 77 of the Copyright,
Designs and Patents Act 1988.

Text copyright © Gino D'Acampo 2010
Design © Kyle Books 2010
Photography © Kate Whitaker 2010

Design Nicky Collings
Photography Kate Whitaker
Project Editor Vicky Orchard
Food stylist Nicole Herft
Props stylist Wei Tang
Copy editor Stephanie Evans
Production Gemma John

Colour reproduction by Chromographics
Printed and bound in China by C&C Offset

Acknowledgements
A massive thank you goes to my long-term
publisher Kyle Cathie who once again trusted me
to write my fourth book.

To my manager and friend Jeremy and everybody
at Jeremy Hicks Associates for all their hard work
and commitment on all of my projects – I'm truly
grateful.

Special thanks goes to my favourite photographer
Kate Whitaker and all the team in charge who
made this book so beautiful. Vicky and Nicky – you
did a great job!

A big kiss and a big thank you goes to my food
stylist Nicole Herft and her assistant Simone for
making the food look amazing.

To everybody at Bontà Italia: Marco, Lina, Franco,
Loredana, Leo and Graziana for their continuous
support and patience – it's great to know you're
always there for me.

Of course all this would have been impossible
without the help of my family, Luciano, Rocco and
Jessie, thank you for making my life so beautiful.

Last but not least, a big thank you to Contessa
Maria Teresa Boselli Vespignani for providing her
beautiful villa in Italy where we shot the book.
www.agrivillelacollina.com

Grazie, grazie, grazie to you for once again
choosing my book, enjoy and *Buon Appetito!*
www.ginodacampo.com
Twitter page - @ginofantastico

CONTENTS

Gino's Introduction **6**

The Nutritional Benefits of Pasta **8**

Gino's Tips for Perfect Pasta **14**

Fresh & Filled Pasta **16**

Dried Pasta **50**

Baked & Sweet Pasta **82**

Like Mamma Used to Make **112**

Pasta on the Go **148**

Pasta for those with Allergies **176**

Index **206**

INTRODUCTION

Finally it has happened… here I am writing a book dedicated exclusively to pasta – by far my favourite Italian dish ever. I remember, like it was yesterday…I was thirteen on my first day at the catering college. My teacher took me to the kitchen and showed me how to make fresh pasta dough. At that point, I got so excited that I promised myself that one day I would share this experience with as many people as possible. Since then, my love affair with pasta has never changed. If I had my way, I would eat it for breakfast, lunch and dinner.

Growing up, I don't ever remember having a meal with my family where pasta didn't feature, especially Sunday lunch. My mother used to make, and still does, the most beautiful lasagne ever. No matter how big she made it, however, there was never any left over at the end of the meal – in fact, my sister and I used to argue over the last slice. I have carried on this tradition and most Sundays I make sure I enjoy a good plate of pasta with my wife and my boys and it's really funny and lovely to see them, in their turn, arguing over the last portion.

Italy without pasta is like Britain without tea – it's just impossible to picture. We have more than 600 different shapes of pasta and, believe it or not, each has been designed specifically for a particular sauce. Just for the record, in Italy, there is no such thing as *spaghetti* Bolognese, we would always choose tagliatelle or pappardelle as these absorb the flavour of the sauce much better. Of course, let's not forget all the filled pastas that we have, such as ravioli, tortelloni and mezzelune (half-moon shaped pasta), which traditionally are always served with a light sauce (such as butter and fresh sage), mainly because you don't want the sauce to overpower the filling.

Nowadays you can buy a packet of pasta from pretty much every corner shop, but please trust me when I say that if you spend a little extra the end result will be 100 per cent better. The best pasta is made by the traditional method of pressing the dough through a bronze die, which gives it a slightly rough surface that allows the sauce to stick to it. This type of pasta is more expensive but it's truly worth it!

Whichever type you choose, a plate of pasta has to be the ultimate fast food dish. You only have to boil some salted water, cook the pasta for 7–8 minutes, drain and then serve with a drizzle of extra virgin olive oil and a sprinkle of Parmesan cheese and you have a filling, tasty, healthy and inexpensive dish – what more could you want? I can see now why there are references to macaroni dating back to the 13th century; also why the Chinese still maintain it was their discovery. Rubbish! Pasta has to be, and certainly was, the creation of an Italian.

In this book, you will find 100 tasty, stylish yet very simple pasta recipes that can be used for a quick meal or as a course for your dinner party. All the ingredients are widely available, which means you won't need to drive yourself mad finding them. I have also chosen dishes that can be served to children and adults at the same time, just to make dinner a little easier.

All of them demonstrate that you don't need to spend a lot of time in the kitchen to enjoy a great Italian dish and will tell you everything you need to know about cooking the perfect plate of pasta. Of course, *Gino's Pasta* is perfect for my ongoing motto too:

Minimum Effort, Maximum Satisfaction!

Buon Appetito!

THE NUTRITIONAL BENEFITS OF PASTA
By Juliette Kellow BSc RD

Carbohydrate-rich foods like pasta, rice, bread, couscous and potatoes have had a hard time in recent years. For a while, the popularity of low-carb slimming diets turned a delicious plate of spaghetti into the enemy. But fortunately, thanks to continued scientific research, health experts remain convinced that carbs are more friend than foe when it comes to keeping us healthy and staying in shape – providing we choose the right sort and don't eat them in enormous portions.

Of course, it's something true Italians have always known. Screen legend and Hollywood beauty Sophia Loren famously claimed that eating pasta helped to contribute to her youthful looks. 'Everything you see, I owe to spaghetti', she once said. Meanwhile, in her book *Women & Beauty*, she states, 'Italians are lucky to live with a culinary heritage that relies on pasta because it is a complex carbohydrate and a very efficient and healthy fuel for the body'.

Health experts agree. In the UK, the British Dietetic Association (BDA) maintains that starchy foods like pasta are an important part of a healthy, balanced diet and recommends they make up roughly a third of the food we eat. The BDA confirms that omitting starchy foods from our diet can be bad for our health because we could miss

out on a range of nutrients. What's more, the BDA verifies that low-carb diets tend to be higher in fat, which could increase our risk of coronary heart disease. Plus they also reduce fibre, which may help to reduce the risk of cancer.

Other countries in the Western world are of the same opinion. Health guidelines throughout Europe, Australia, New Zealand and America recommend that starchy foods, together with fruit and vegetables, form the majority of our diet.

Meanwhile, the idea that carbs like pasta are 'fattening' is something of a myth. Basically, it's an excess of calories that makes us pile on the pounds – and it really doesn't matter where these extra calories come from. There's certainly no good evidence to suggest that carbs are solely responsible for the nation's expanding waistlines – or that, if we want to lose weight, a low-carb diet is the best way to achieve it. Indeed, research shows that in the long term, there's no significant difference in the amount of weight lost by people following either a low-carbohydrate or low-calorie diet.

Furthermore, carbs actually contain half the calories of fat – a gram of pure carbohydrate provides just 4 calories, compared to 9 calories in a gram of pure fat! Ultimately, it's what you serve carbs with that can pile on the calories. More often than not, the fat we add to carbs is what boosts the calorie content. For example, a 230g serving of cooked spaghetti contains just 239 calories. Mixing it with 2 tablespoons of olive oil adds an extra 200 calories – almost doubling the calories of the dish.

PASTA PERFECTION FOR WAISTLINES

When it comes to choosing which carbs to eat, pasta is a great choice. Like many other starchy foods, pasta is naturally low in fat and saturated fat, and is an important source of energy. But – unlike some other carbs – it releases its energy slowly and steadily, thanks to its low glycaemic index, or GI. The glycaemic index measures the effect different carbohydrate-containing foods have on our blood sugar levels. Foods with a low GI release sugar into the blood slowly, providing us with a steady supply of energy that leaves us satisfied for longer and so less likely to snack. By contrast, foods with a high GI cause a rapid, but short lived, rise in blood sugar followed by a sudden crash. As a result, we quickly feel low on energy and hungry again, meaning that we're more likely to snack, especially on sugary foods, to give us a quick boost. Over time, this frequent snacking can lead to unwanted weight gain. Health experts agree that it's better to choose a diet that contains carbohydrate-rich foods with a low to medium GI because they help to keep us fuller for longer.

It's good news then that pasta has a lower GI than many other starchy foods that are traditionally eaten as an accompaniment to main courses. According to the GI scale, both white and wholewheat varieties of pasta are

COOK 'AL DENTE'

To help ensure pasta keeps us full for as long as possible, it's important to avoid overcooking it. The reason pasta has such a low GI is because the starch granules become 'trapped' in the pasta dough mixture when it is made. Cooking starts to release these starch granules, making it easier for the body's digestive processes to break them down into sugars. More of the starches remain 'trapped' in pasta that is cooked for a shorter time, which is why Gino stresses you cook your pasta so it is al dente or 'firm to the bite'. As a result, lightly cooked pasta makes the digestive system work harder to break the starches into sugars, which in turn slows the release of these sugars into the bloodstream. Ultimately, al dente pasta has a lower GI than soft, soggy pasta that's been overcooked, and so will help to stave off any hunger pangs to keep you feeling fuller for longer. As a rule of thumb, try cooking your pasta for 1 minute less than the packet instructions recommend.

classified as having a low GI. In comparison, boiled potatoes, basmati and brown rice and couscous have a medium GI, whilst mashed and jacket potatoes, white and wholemeal bread and white rice all have a high GI. Bottom line: pasta is likely to keep us feeling satisfied and fuller for longer than many other popular starchy foods, making it easier for us to control our weight – and lose any excess pounds if necessary.

But foods with a low GI don't just help us to keep our waistlines in good shape. Many studies have revealed that diets containing plenty of low GI foods may also help to protect us from a range of diseases. Australian scientists, for example, recently reviewed 37 studies that had looked at low GI diets and the risk of chronic disease. In 2008, they published their findings in the *American Journal of Clinical Nutrition* and concluded that people with the lowest GI diets were the least likely to suffer with type 2

HEALTHY PASTA LEFTOVERS

Storing leftover pasta in the fridge overnight and using it to make a pasta salad for lunch the next day is a great way to further lower its GI. This is because the cooking and cooling process alters the structure of the starch in the pasta, causing some of it to resist digestion. This 'resistant starch' is not digested and so does not break down into its component sugars. This means cooked and quickly cooled pasta has less impact on our blood sugar levels and so has an even lower GI than pasta that's eaten immediately after cooking. Resistant starch passes into the large intestine where it provides 'food' for good bacteria, which help to keep our immune and digestive systems healthy and in good working order.

diabetes, coronary heart disease, gall-bladder disease and breast cancer.

WHOLEWHEAT GOODNESS

Whilst all pasta is low in fat and a good source of starchy carbs, as the chart shows, wholewheat pasta is a richer source of fibre and nutrients than white pasta. This is because it is made from the whole of the wheat grain, including the nutrient-rich germ, the energy-providing endosperm and the fibre-rich bran layer. When wheat grains are refined, the outer bran layer and germ of the grain are stripped away, so the grain loses much of its fibre and many of its vitamins, minerals and antioxidants. Together with starchy carbohydrates, it is this package of nutrients in wholegrain foods such as wholewheat pasta that is thought to be linked to good health.

Pasta Nutrition Know-How

Nutrient	Cooked white spaghetti (per 230g serving)	Recommended intakes for adults (%)	Cooked wholewheat spaghetti (per 230g serving)	Recommended intakes for adults (%)
Energy (kcal)	239	12	260	13
Protein (g)	8.3	18	10.8	24
Fat (g)	1.6	2	2.1	3
Of which saturates (g)	0.2	1	0.2	1
Carbohydrates (g)	51.1	22	53.4	23
Of which sugars (g)	1.2	1	3	3
Fibre (g)	2.8	16	8.1	45
Salt (g)	0	0	0.1	2
Minerals				
Potassium (mg)	55	3	322	16
Magnesium (mg)	35	9	97	26
Phosphorus (mg)	101	14	253	36
Iron (mg)	1.2	9	3.2	23
Copper (mg)	0.2	20	0.4	40
Zinc (mg)	1.2	12	2.5	25
Manganese (mg)	0.7	35	2.1	105
Vitamins				
Thiamin (mg)	0.02	2	0.48	44
Niacin equivalents (mg)	2.8	18	5.3	33

A typical serving of wholewheat spaghetti contains almost three times the fibre of white spaghetti and provides almost half the recommended daily fibre intake for adults.

In fact, many studies have shown that wholegrain foods can help to keep us slim and protect us from disease. For example, in one study that looked at the diets of more than 74,000 female nurses over a 12-year period, the women who ate the most wholegrains consistently weighed less than those who ate the least – and were half as likely to gain weight. There's also good evidence to suggest that adults who eat more wholegrain foods are less likely to suffer with insulin resistance (a precursor for type 2 diabetes) and heart disease. Other research shows that a good, regular intake of wholegrains helps to keep the digestive system healthy, prevents gallstones, and reduces the risk of developing breast and colon cancer.

A PERFECT PARTNER

Pasta provides a fantastic foundation for putting together a balanced, nutritious meal. To help people create healthy meals, most health organisations throughout the Western world recommend eating fewer fatty and sugary foods, in favour of choosing most of our food intake from the following groups:

• Starchy foods such as pasta, bread, rice and potatoes
• Fruit and vegetables
• Protein-rich foods such as meat, fish, eggs and beans
• Dairy products such as milk, cheese and yogurt

Using pasta as the base for meals, it is easy to add ingredients from each of the other main food groups. For example, serving pasta with a classic Bolognese sauce

KEY NUTRIENTS IN PASTA

Potassium - Potassium works with sodium to control the balance of fluids in the body. It is also needed to conduct nerve impulses, initiate muscle contractions and regulate heartbeat and blood pressure.

Magnesium - This mineral clots blood and is needed for strong bones and teeth. It is involved in energy production, nerve function and muscle relaxation and helps to regulate the rhythm of the heart.

Phosphorus - Phosphorus is needed for strong bones and teeth and is important for energy production and healthy cells.

Iron - Iron is needed for healthy blood, is a component of many enzymes and helps keep the immune system healthy.

Copper - This nutrient is important for immunity and keeping the heart healthy. It is also a component of collagen – a protein in bones, skin and connective tissue.

Zinc - Zinc is essential for normal growth, enzyme function, wound healing, fertility and for keeping the immune system strong to fight infection.

Manganese - Manganese is important for healthy bones and brain function and is needed to produce sex hormones.

Vitamin B1 (thiamin) - This vitamin releases the energy from nutrients, keeps the heart healthy and is essential for a healthy nervous system, growth in children and fertility in adults.

Vitamin B3 (niacin) - This vitamin also releases the energy from nutrients and helps to control blood sugar levels. It keeps skin healthy and ensures the nervous and digestive systems function properly.

PASTA DO'S AND DON'TS

Don't...

- Overcook pasta – keep it 'al dente' to keep the GI low
- Discard leftover pasta – cold pasta has a lower GI than hot pasta and is perfect for making salads
- Add too much salt to the cooking water – health experts say adults should have no more than 6g salt a day
- Use oil in the cooking water – as well as adding extra calories and fat, it means your sauce won't stick to the surface of the pasta as easily

Do...

- Choose your sauce wisely – for a healthy meal opt for a low-fat sauce such as a classic tomato sauce made from a little olive oil, onions, garlic, herbs and tomatoes
- Try wholewheat pasta – it now comes in lots of different varieties, including penne, fusilli and spaghetti
- Add lots of vegetables to pasta – or include them in sauces
- Stick to sensible portions – no more than 230g cooked pasta (around 100g uncooked)

that includes tomatoes, mushrooms and carrots (from fruit and veg) and lean mince (from protein-rich foods), topped off with a sprinkling of Parmesan (from dairy products) provides a well-balanced, nutritious meal that is in line with the healthy eating guidelines of most countries in the West.

In particular, pasta is a great vehicle for adding more vegetables to our diet, helping us to achieve our 5-a-day. A whole host of vegetables can be added to (or hidden in!) pasta sauces – especially good news for fussy eaters who love pasta but are less keen on eating vegetables.

Indeed, many of the recipes in this book are great examples of how pasta-based meals can help us to eat more veg in a tasty way. Each serving of Gino's Tagliatelle Primavera (see page 33), provides two of your 5-a-day – add a salad and you're more than halfway there!

Pasta is also a great choice for people who follow a vegetarian diet – protein-rich alternatives to meat and fish, such as beans and nuts, are perfect for partnering with pasta in a sauce or salad. Finally, even people with an intolerance to wheat or gluten can enjoy pasta these days, thanks to an increasingly wide range of pastas based on corn, rice and even quinoa (see chapter 6).

GINO'S TIPS FOR PERFECT PASTA

The most common question I get asked about cooking pasta is if there is ever any need to add oil to the boiling water. The answer is very simple: NEVER drizzle oil into the water when you cook pasta – it is a waste of both time and money. Oil is lighter than water and therefore when you add it into the boiling water it rises to the surface, so it doesn't prevent the pasta sticking together because the pasta stays below it.

What will help the pasta not to stick to each other is the bubbles in the boiling water that constantly move the pasta around the pan. Make sure you always have a big saucepan when you are cooking pasta, usually I would suggest a 24cm diameter saucepan at least 20cm tall, which will enable you to cook 1kg of pasta at a time.

You should never cook more than a kilo of pasta at a time, otherwise it can be difficult to prevent the pasta sticking together. For every 500g of dried or fresh pasta, you need at least 4.5 litres of water and for every 4.5 litres of water you will need two heaped tablespoons of salt. Of course bear in mind that if you are making a sauce that will make the pasta more salty, such as one using anchovies, capers or olives, you will not need as much salt in the boiling water, so perhaps cut to one heaped tablespoon instead.

In my family we always calculate 120g of dried pasta per serving, therefore we usually use a packet of 500g for four people. Of course you can use less but more would be very greedy.

If I had to choose the best tools to cook a great pasta dish they would be :

- **A large pot**
- **A large colander/sieve** for draining the cooked pasta
- **A long pair of tongs**, which are useful for any long-shaped pasta
- **A long wooden spoon**, which can be used to stir the pasta and the sauce that you are preparing.

- **A large frying pan or saucepan** to make the sauce – it is important to allow the sauce to coat the pasta before serving it and you therefore need enough space to stir them together comfortably.

Cooking the pasta in a saucepan of boiling water with the lid on can be another common mistake, simply because eventually the water will overflow making a big mess in your kitchen. If you want to get the perfect al dente bite, cook the pasta for one minute less than instructed on the packet.

One of the biggest secrets to making a perfect plate of pasta is to make sure that the sauce is ready before you start cooking the pasta, otherwise the pasta will be cooked and start to become soggy while waiting for the sauce to cook.

There are more than 600 different varieties of pasta and in Italy we use each shape with a specific sauce, for example farfalline (little bows), diatalini (little fingers) and stelline (little stars) are used mainly in soups as they are smaller. Linguine is used with seafood sauces and farfalle, maccheroni, tagliatelle and fettuccine are usually accompanied with traditional tomato-based sauces. If you like creamy sauces make sure that you use a pasta with ridges like penne rigate or fusilli so that the sauce sticks to the pasta.

If you are making filled pasta, such as ravioli, mezzelune or tortelloni, remember that you can freeze it. Simply place a single layer of the filled pasta on a tray sprinkled with flour or semolina and place in the freezer making sure they don't touch one another while they freeze. Once frozen, the shapes can be put into plastic bags and stored for up to five months. To cook the frozen pasta, allow a minute longer than usual as the heat of the water needs to pass into the frozen fillings.

GINO'S **TOP TEN PASTA TIPS**

1 To cook the perfect pasta, you should always make sure that you have enough water in the saucepan. You need 4.5 litres of water to cook 500g of pasta.

2 Make sure that the water is always *bollente* (fast boiling) before you start cooking the pasta.

3 For every 4.5 litres of water, you will need two heaped tablespoons of salt.

4 Never ever cook pasta with the lid on the saucepan.

5 Stir the pasta into the boiling water at least every two minutes during cooking.

6 There is never any need to put oil into the boiling water before you cook the pasta – it's just a waste of time and money.

7 Make sure the pasta is always cooked al dente (firm to the bite) – so keep tasting as you cook.

8 Remember that fresh pasta always cooks faster than dried varieties.

9 When making pasta dough, make sure you do not overknead it, otherwise the dough will get warm and will be more difficult to stretch.

10 The most important rule of all – always make sure that the pasta is coated in the sauce and never just place the sauce on top of the pasta.

FRESH & FILLED PASTA

MAKING PASTA
Homemade egg pasta dough

I know you may think that this is complicated and very fiddly, but please promise me that at some point you will try it. I can assure you that when you've made your fresh pasta dough once you will definitely do it again. You really will feel satisfied making a dish completely from scratch – have a go – you won't be disappointed.

Makes about 400g
300g white flour, type '00', plus extra for dusting
3 medium eggs
1/2 teaspoon fine salt
1 tablespoon extra virgin olive oil

1 Sift the flour onto your work surface. Make a well in the centre and break in the eggs. Add in the salt and oil.

2 Using the handle of a wooden spoon, mix the flour into the eggs, working from the centre outwards. Once you have a crumbly texture, gather the mixture together with your hands and start to knead until you have a soft dough.

3 Once the dough has come together, continue to knead for about 8 minutes, using both hands, exactly as if you were kneading bread.

4 Roll the dough into a ball, cover with cling film and leave to rest in the fridge for 20 minutes.

5 Once the dough has rested, simply flatten it with your fingers so that it can fit through the rollers of the pasta machine.

6 Flour the pasta lightly on both sides and start to roll it through the pasta machine from the widest setting to the thinnest. Make sure you keep the pasta dusted with flour at all times.

VARIATIONS
Green pasta: Cook 225g fresh spinach, drain thoroughly then purée in a food processor. Add with the eggs.

Tomato pasta: Add 2 tablespoons tomato purée with the eggs.

FRESH EGG TAGLIATELLE

Makes about 100g

1 Prepare the dough as described on page 19 and remove from the fridge after resting.

2 Once the dough has rested, simply flatten it with your fingers so that it can fit through the rollers of the pasta machine.

3 Flour the pasta lightly on both sides and start to roll it through the pasta machine from the widest setting to the thinnest. Make sure you keep the pasta dusted with flour at all times. Then roll the pasta through the tagliatelle cutting attachment, gently lifting the strands as you do so.

4 If you do not have a pasta machine you can cut the tagliatelle by hand. Dust the work surface, the dough and the rolling pin with flour to prevent sticking.

5 Start by flattening the dough with the palm of your hand, then place the rolling pin across the dough and roll it towards the centre. Continue to roll the pin back and forth turning the dough every so often.

6 At this point the dough should spread out and flatten evenly. When it is thin enough to see your fingers through it, it's ready.

7 Start to fold the pasta sheet like a flattened cigar from one edge to the centre, and then repeat from the other edge to the centre.

8 Use a well-floured, long sharp knife to cut the rolled dough into 5mm wide strips.

9 Slide the knife beneath the rolled pasta sheet, lining up the edge of the knife with the centre of the folds. Gently lift up the knife and the pasta ribbons will fall down on each side.

10 Toss the tagliatelle in a little more flour and cook within the hour.

PAPPARDELLE ALLO ZAFFERANO
Fresh saffron pappardelle

The earthy flavour of the saffron mixed into the pasta dough is a delicious combination. It will make your pasta very very yellow, which will add to the look as well as the flavour. Make sure you do not overknead the dough, otherwise it will become warm and therefore difficult to stretch into the pasta machine.

Makes about 400g pappardelle
3 medium eggs
6 x 0.125g sachets saffron powder
300g white flour, type '00', plus extra for dusting
1/2 teaspoon fine salt
1 tablespoon extra virgin olive oil

1 Lightly beat the eggs with the saffron powder in a medium bowl.

2 Sift the flour into a large bowl. Make a well in the centre and add the beaten eggs, salt and oil.

3 Using the handle of a wooden spoon, mix the flour into the eggs, working from the centre outwards. Once you have a crumbly texture, turn out the mixture onto a well-floured surface and start to knead until you have a soft dough.

4 Once the dough has come together, continue to knead for about 8 minutes using both hands, exactly as if you were kneading bread.

5 Roll the dough into a ball, cover with cling film and leave to rest in the fridge for 20 minutes.

6 Dust the work surface, the dough and the rolling pin with flour to prevent sticking.

7 Start by flattening the dough with the palm of your hand, then place the rolling pin across the dough and roll it towards the centre. Continue to roll the pin back and forth turning the dough every so often.

8 At this point the dough should spread out and flatten evenly. When it is thin enough to see your fingers through it, it's ready.

9 Start to fold the pasta sheet like a flattened cigar from one edge to the centre, and then repeat from the other edge to the centre.

10 Use a long sharp knife to cut the rolled dough into 1.5cm wide strips.

11 Slide the knife beneath the rolled pasta sheet, lining up the edge of the knife with the centre of the folds.

12 Gently lift up the knife and the pasta ribbons will fall down on each side.

13 Toss the pappardelle in a little more flour and cook within the hour.

14 Cook in a large saucepan of boiling salted water for 2–3 minutes until al dente.

MEZZELUNE DI ZUCCA E NOCI
Pasta filled with roasted butternut squash and walnuts

This has to be the queen of all filled pasta. The combination of butternut squash with walnuts and thyme is absolutely lovely. If you prefer, you can substitute the walnuts with pine nuts and make sure you use a good-quality Italian extra virgin olive oil to drizzle over the pasta.

Serves 6
400g fresh egg pasta dough, see page 19

2 eggs, beaten
200ml extra virgin olive oil
100g freshly grated Parmesan cheese

For the filling
1 butternut squash, about 700g
3 tablespoons extra virgin olive oil
4 tablespoons finely chopped walnuts
3 tablespoons freshly grated Parmesan cheese
3 tablespoons finely chopped raisins
2 tablespoons finely chopped fresh thyme leaves,
  plus extra to serve
salt and pepper to taste

1 Preheat the oven to 200°C/fan 180°C/gas mark 6.

2 Peel the butternut squash, cut in half and remove the seeds and fibres. Chop into 3cm cubes and place on a baking tray.

3 Drizzle over 3 tablespoons of extra virgin olive oil and roast in the oven for 1 hour until soft and coloured. Remove from the oven and allow to cool. Place the butternut squash in a food processor and blitz until creamy. Pour the purée into a sieve and leave for 1 hour to allow any excess water to drain. Place the purée in a bowl and fold in the remaining ingredients for the filling. Season with salt and pepper.

4 Gradually roll out the dough in a pasta machine to its thinnest setting. Make sure you continuously dust the sheets with a little flour otherwise they can get sticky.

5 Lay the pasta sheets on a well-floured surface. Cut into discs using an 8cm cutter – you should get 28–30 discs.

6 Place about a teaspoonful of filling in the middle of each disc, sharing it out equally. Brush the edges of the discs with beaten egg and fold over to make a half-moon shape. Press down to seal with your fingertips. Using a fork, press the edges again to secure the filling.

7 Cook the mezzelune in a large saucepan of boiling salted water for 1 minute (work in batches if necessary), drain and place in the middle of a large serving plate.

8 Season with a little salt and pepper. Drizzle over the extra virgin olive oil, sprinkle with the Parmesan cheese and a little thyme and serve immediately.

FETTUCCINE AL RAGÙ

Fettuccine with meat and red wine sauce

A traditional Italian ragù sauce will take you a good twenty hours of cooking and you will need more than twenty five ingredients to prepare it. This is not the case for this recipe but trust me, there is no compromise as far as flavours are concerned. If you prefer you can substitute the minced pork with lamb for a variation.

Serves 6

4 tablespoons olive oil
1 onion, peeled and finely chopped
1 large carrot, peeled and grated
2 celery sticks, finely chopped
500g minced beef
500g minced pork
2 glasses of dry red wine
700ml passata (sieved tomatoes)
2 tablespoons tomato purée
200ml chicken stock
500g fresh fettuccine or egg tagliatelle, see page 21
salt and pepper to taste

1 Heat the olive oil in a large saucepan and cook the onion, carrot and celery for 5 minutes over a medium heat, stirring occasionally with a wooden spoon.

2 Add in the minced meats and continue to cook for a further 5 minutes, stirring continuously until coloured all over. Season with salt and pepper.

3 Pour in the wine, stir well and continue to cook for 5 minutes until the wine has evaporated.

4 Pour in the passata with the tomato purée and the stock, lower the heat and cook, uncovered, for 2 hours. Stir the sauce every 20 minutes to prevent it from sticking.

5 Once the sauce is ready, remove from the heat, season with salt and pepper and set aside.

6 Cook the pasta in a large saucepan of boiling salted water until al dente. Drain and tip back into the same pan.

7 Put the saucepan back over a low heat, pour in the ragù sauce and gently stir everything together for 30 seconds to allow the flavours to combine.

8 Serve hot.

TAGLIATELLE CON GAMBERI E BRANDY
Tagliatelle with prawns and a creamy brandy sauce

This is the ideal plate of pasta for a first date or if you need to be forgiven. It's delicate, full of flavours and very impressive. You can substitute the brandy with Marsala wine and please make sure you don't overcook the prawns.

Serves 4
30g salted butter
4 tablespoons olive oil
2 shallots, peeled and finely chopped
60g walnuts, chopped
300g uncooked prawns, peeled
10 cherry tomatoes, quartered
60ml brandy
250ml double cream
1 tablespoon balsamic vinegar
400g fresh egg tagliatelle, see page 21
2 tablespoons freshly chopped flat leaf parsley
salt and pepper to taste

1 Melt the butter with the oil in a large frying pan over a low heat and fry the shallots and walnuts for 2 minutes, stirring occasionally with a wooden spoon.

2 Increase the heat to medium, add the prawns and tomatoes, season with salt and pepper and continue to cook for 30 seconds.

3 Pour in the brandy and continue to cook for a further minute to allow the alcohol to evaporate.

4 Add the cream with the balsamic vinegar and cook, stirring, for 2 minutes. Set aside.

5 Meanwhile cook the pasta in a large saucepan of boiling salted water until al dente. Drain and tip back into the same pan.

6 Pour in the cream sauce with the parsley and toss everything together for 30 seconds to allow the flavours to combine.

7 Serve immediately.

FETTUCCINE CON POLLO E DOLCELATTE
Fettuccine with chicken and Dolcelatte

On Italian menus there is often an option of baked penne with a creamy chicken sauce. From this I created what I feel is the ultimate chicken pasta. Adding the wine, chives and Dolcelatte cheese gives the meat an amazing flavour and putting it with fettuccine works brilliantly. It's a really hearty meal and will leave you completely satisfied. If you prefer, you can substitute Dolcelatte with Gorgonzola cheese.

Serves 4

2 tablespoons olive oil

350g boneless and skinless chicken breast, cut into thin strips

200g Dolcelatte cheese, cut into chunks

150ml double cream

50ml dry white wine

3 tablespoons freshly chopped chives

400g fresh fettuccine or egg tagliatelle, see page 21

salt and pepper to taste

1 Heat the oil in a medium saucepan over a medium heat and fry the chicken for 6 minutes until golden all over, stirring occasionally with a wooden spoon. Add the Dolcelatte to the pan, lower the heat and cook for 2 minutes, stirring until melted.

2 Pour in the cream and wine and continue to cook for a further minute, stirring continuously.

3 Mix in the chives and season with salt and plenty of black pepper. Set aside.

4 Meanwhile cook the pasta in a large saucepan of boiling salted water until al dente. Drain and tip back into the same pan.

5 Pour in the creamy chicken sauce and stir everything together for 30 seconds to allow the sauce to coat the pasta evenly.

6 Serve immediately.

TAGLIATELLE PRIMAVERA

Spicy tagliatelle with peppers, courgettes, red onions and thyme

I never want to hear from anyone that it's hard to cook for a vegetarian. I know if you are a meat lover it can be annoying but there are some amazing pasta dishes out there that you can cook and this is one of them. Peppers, courgettes and onions are a great combination of vegetables and with a small punch of chilli, make this meal delicious. You can substitute fettuccine instead of tagliatelle if you prefer and make sure you don't overcook the vegetables.

Serves 4

8 tablespoons olive oil

2 red onions, peeled and finely sliced

2 yellow peppers, halved, deseeded and chopped
   into 1cm cubes

1 red pepper, halved, deseeded and chopped
   into 1cm cubes

1 courgette, trimmed and chopped into 1cm cubes

1/2 teaspoon dried chilli flakes

1 tablespoon fresh thyme leaves

400g fresh egg tagliatelle, see page 21

salt to taste

1 Heat the oil in a large frying pan over a medium heat and fry the onions, peppers, courgettes, chilli and thyme for 8 minutes. Stir occasionally with a wooden spoon. Season with salt and set aside.

2 Meanwhile cook the pasta in a large saucepan of boiling salted water until al dente. Drain and tip back into the same pan.

3 Pour in the sauce, place the pan over a low heat and toss everything together for 30 seconds to allow the flavours to combine.

4 Divide the pasta between four serving plates and serve immediately.

TAGLIATELLE IN SALSA TARTARA
Tagliatelle in creamy tartare sauce

For anyone like me who loves the flavour of pickled gherkins, onions and capers, this is definitely the pasta dish for you. Of course my inspiration came from the famous tartare sauce to which a little double cream is added – it works beautifully with fresh tagliatelle. You can substitute the tagliatelle with spaghetti or linguine if you prefer but please make sure that they are cooked al dente.

Serves 4

60g small pickled onions
60g little pickled gherkins
30g salted capers, rinsed under cold water
30g salted butter
150g double cream
1 teaspoon English mustard
400g fresh egg tagliatelle, see page 21
2 egg yolks
4 tablespoons freshly chopped flat leaf parsley
4 tablespoons freshly grated Parmesan cheese
salt and pepper to taste

1 Drain the onions and the gherkins from the vinegar and place on a chopping board with the capers. Roughly chop.

2 Place the butter in a large frying pan over a medium heat and fry the chopped onions, gherkins and capers together for 2 minutes.

3 Pour in the cream and mustard, mix well and continue to cook gently for a further 3 minutes. Season with salt and pepper and stir occasionally.

4 Meanwhile cook the pasta in a large saucepan of boiling salted water until al dente.

5 Drain and tip into the frying pan with the creamy sauce. Add the egg yolks and sprinkle in the parsley. Toss everything together on a low heat for 15 seconds to allow the sauce to coat the pasta.

6 Divide the pasta between four serving plates and serve immediately, topped with the Parmesan cheese.

FETTUCCINE ALLE CIPOLLE
Fettuccine with sweet onions, rosemary and minced lamb

I am begging you to try this one – it's a must! This recipe is so easy to prepare – adding in the wine and stock gives the lamb such a lovely flavour and the onions create a truly creamy texture. Even thinking about this dish makes my mouth water. In fact, I paused through writing this intro to make this very dish. Think roast lamb with fresh rosemary, sautéed onions and a glass of wine. Imagine those flavours and now add pasta – heaven.

Serves 4
6 tablespoons olive oil
3 large onions, peeled and finely sliced
1 carrot, peeled and finely grated
1 tablespoon freshly chopped rosemary
200g minced lamb
200ml white wine
300ml vegetable stock
400g fresh fettuccine or egg tagliatelle, see page 21
100g freshly grated Parmesan cheese
salt and pepper to taste

1 Heat the olive oil in a large saucepan and fry the onions, carrot and rosemary for 5 minutes over a medium heat until softened and golden. Stir occasionally with a wooden spoon.

2 Add the lamb and mix well allowing the meat to crumble. Continue to cook for 5 minutes stirring frequently until the meat has browned all over.

3 Pour in the wine and cook for a further 3 minutes to allow the alcohol to evaporate. Season with salt and pepper and pour in the stock. Bring to the boil then lower the heat and simmer, uncovered, for 30 minutes. Stir every 10 minutes.

4 Meanwhile cook the pasta in a large saucepan of boiling salted water until al dente.

5 Drain the pasta and immediately add to the meat sauce. Increase the heat to high and gently mix the sauce and the pasta together for 30 seconds to allow the sauce to coat the pasta evenly. Stir constantly.

6 Serve immediately, topped with the freshly grated Parmesan cheese.

MEZZELUNE CON PROSCIUTTO E POMODORI SECCHI
Half-moon shaped pasta filled with ham and sun-dried tomatoes

In the D'Acampo family we adore making fresh filled pasta and this recipe is one of our top ten must-have meals. If you fancy, substitute the cooked ham with Parma ham.

Serves 6
200ml extra virgin olive oil
200g chorizo, cut into 0.5cm slices
400g fresh egg pasta dough, see page 19
2 eggs, beaten
100g piece of Pecorino cheese

For the filling
750g ricotta cheese
200g cooked ham, finely chopped
150g sun-dried tomatoes in oil, drained and chopped
15 fresh basil leaves, chopped
100g freshly grated Pecorino cheese
salt and pepper to taste

1 Place all the ingredients for the filling in a large bowl and mix together with a fork. Season with salt and pepper. Cover with cling film and leave to rest in the fridge for 10 minutes.

2 Meanwhile put the extra virgin olive oil in a frying pan over a medium heat and fry the chorizo for 3 minutes, stirring occasionally. Set aside.

3 Flatten the prepared pasta dough with your fingers so that it can fit through the rollers of the pasta machine. Flour the pasta lightly on both sides and start to roll it from the widest setting to the thinnest. Make sure you keep the pasta dusted with flour at all times.

4 Lay the pasta sheets on a well-floured surface. Cut into discs using an 8cm cutter – you should get 28–30 discs. Place about a teaspoonful of filling in the middle of each disc, sharing it out equally. Brush the edges of the discs with beaten egg and fold over to make a half-moon shape. Press down to seal with your fingertips. Using a fork, press the edges again to secure the filling.

5 Cook the mezzelune in a large saucepan of boiling salted water for 1 minute (work in batches if necessary), drain and place in the middle of a large serving plate. Season with a little salt and pepper.

6 Top with the chorizo and the oil, sprinkle with shavings of Pecorino cheese and serve immediately.

TAGLIATELLE AL TARTUFO
Tagliatelle served with butter and truffle shavings

I have to admit that this is probably the most expensive recipe in this book as I'm using the most luxurious ingredient you can buy, truffle. My best friend Marco is obsessed with this plate of pasta and of course whenever I have the chance to make it he always gets the first invite. Whatever you do, please make sure you never buy truffle preserved in brine. You must only use fresh truffle, otherwise please don't try this recipe, because you will be disappointed.

Serves 4
80g salted butter
400g fresh egg tagliatelle, see page 21
1 small white or black truffle
60g freshly grated Parmesan cheese
salt and pepper to taste

1 Melt the butter in a large frying pan with plenty of black pepper. Set aside.

2 Meanwhile cook the pasta in a large saucepan of boiling salted water until al dente. Drain and tip into the frying pan with the butter. Season with salt and toss together for 10 seconds allowing the butter to coat evenly the pasta.

3 Divide the tagliatelle between four serving plates and shave over the fresh truffle.

4 Sprinkle the top with Parmesan cheese and serve immediately.

RAVIOLI CON RICOTTA E SALMONE
Ravioli with ricotta cheese and smoked salmon

I was sixteen on my first trip to England when I got my first job in Guildford in a very exclusive Italian restaurant. I can still remember like it was yesterday the flavour and the smell of this beautiful pasta dish. I know you may think that it's a bit fiddly to prepare but please believe me, once you've tried it, it will be part of your life forever. Enjoy!

Serves 6
400g fresh egg pasta dough, see page 19
2 eggs, beaten
200ml extra virgin olive oil
3 tablespoons finely chopped fresh chives

For the filling
750g ricotta cheese
zest of 2 unwaxed lemons
300g smoked salmon, chopped
3 tablespoons finely chopped fresh chives
salt and pepper to taste

1 Place all the ingredients for the filling in a large bowl and mix together with a fork. Season with salt and pepper. Cover with cling film and leave to rest in the fridge for 10 minutes.

2 Flatten the prepared dough with your fingers so that it can fit through the rollers of the pasta machine. Flour the pasta lightly on both sides and start to roll it from the widest setting to the thinnest. Make sure you keep the pasta dusted with flour at all times.

3 Lay the pasta sheets on a well-floured surface. Put teaspoonfuls of filling at 4cm intervals across half of the rolled out dough. Brush the spaces between the fillings with the beaten egg. Gently cover with the other half of the dough and press down between the parcels of filling on all sides.

4 Use a pastry wheel or sharp knife to cut the pasta into squares between the fillings.

5 Cook the ravioli in a large saucepan of boiling salted water for 3 minutes (work in batches if necessary), drain and place in the middle of a large serving plate. Season with a little salt and pepper.

6 Drizzle over the extra virgin olive oil, sprinkle with the chives and serve immediately.

PAPPARDELLE DI ZAFFERANO AI FUNGHI
Saffron pappardelle with Marsala and mushrooms

I learnt how to make saffron pappardelle in a very famous restaurant in Bologna. Since then, I must have done this recipe at least a hundred times. The earthy flavour of the saffron in the fresh pappardelle is just spectacular and served with Marsala wine and mushrooms it's at its best. Please make sure you don't overcook the pappardelle.

Serves 4
60g salted butter
4 tablespoons olive oil
2 red onions, peeled and finely chopped
200g button mushrooms, quartered
50ml Marsala wine
150ml double cream
2 tablespoons freshly chopped flat leaf parsley
400g fresh saffron pappardelle, see page 22
salt and pepper to taste

1 Melt the butter in the oil in a large frying pan over a low heat and fry the onions for 3 minutes, stirring occasionally with a wooden spoon.

2 Add in the mushrooms, season with salt and pepper and continue to cook for 5 minutes, stirring occasionally.

3 Pour in the Marsala wine and cook for a further minute to allow the alcohol to evaporate.

4 Pour in the cream with the parsley, stir everything together and cook for 1 minute over a low heat. Set aside, away from the heat.

5 Meanwhile cook the pasta in a large saucepan of boiling salted water until al dente. Drain and tip back into the same pan.

6 Pour in the mushroom sauce and toss everything together for 30 seconds to allow the flavours to combine.

7 Serve immediately.

RAVIOLI CON CHORIZO PICCANTE
Spicy chorizo and ricotta stuffed ravioli

For some reason I am finding chorizo in our fridge every week this year. My wife, Jessie, loves them in her salads so I tried to come up with something special for her. I got lots of loving for this one, so I hope it has the same effect for you!

Serves 6
400g fresh egg pasta dough, see page 19
2 eggs, beaten
200ml extra virgin olive oil

For the filling
5 tablespoons olive oil
300g chorizo, finely chopped
3 medium-hot red chillies, halved, deseeded and finely chopped
750g ricotta cheese
3 tablespoons freshly chopped flat leaf parsley
salt and pepper to taste

1 To prepare the filling, heat the olive oil in a small frying pan over a medium heat and fry the chorizo with the chillies for 2 minutes, stirring occasionally. Set aside.

2 Place the cooled chorizo and chillies in a large bowl with the ricotta and parsley. Mix everything together with a fork and season with salt. Cover with cling film and leave to rest in the fridge for 10 minutes.

3 Flatten the prepared dough with your fingers so that it can fit through the rollers of the pasta machine. Flour the pasta lightly on both sides and start to roll it from the widest setting to the thinnest. Make sure you keep the pasta dusted with flour at all times.

4 Lay the pasta sheets on a well-floured surface. Put teaspoonfuls of filling at 4cm intervals across half the rolled out dough. Brush the spaces between the fillings with the beaten egg. Gently cover with the other half of the dough and press down between the parcels of filling.

5 Use a pastry wheel or sharp knife to cut the pasta into squares between the fillings.

6 Cook the ravioli in a large saucepan of boiling salted water for 3 minutes (work in batches if necessary), drain and place in the middle of a large serving plate. Season with a little salt.

7 Drizzle over the extra virgin olive oil, decorate with plenty of freshly ground black pepper and serve immediately.

TAGLIATELLE CON SALSICCE E PORCINI
Tagliatelle with sausages, rosemary and porcini mushrooms

I love good-quality sausages so this recipe is definitely in my top ten. My grandfather used to make this dish for me when I was a boy but he used a tomato passata instead of the cream that I have introduced. I wish he could have tasted my version as I know I would have got a huge cuddle for this one – he would have loved it and I know that you will too. For those of you who don't like mushrooms, you can leave them out – *Buon Appetito*!

Serves 4
400g Italian sausages or good-quality pork sausages
6 tablespoons olive oil
1 leek, washed and finely chopped
2 tablespoons finely chopped fresh rosemary leaves
50g dried porcini mushrooms, soaked in warm water
  for 15 minutes and drained
100ml dry white wine
150ml double cream
500g fresh egg tagliatelle, see page 21
salt and pepper to taste

1 Remove the skins from the sausages and place the meat mixture in a bowl.

2 Heat the oil in a large frying pan over a low heat and fry the sausage meat and the leek for 5 minutes, stirring occasionally with a wooden spoon to crumble the meat.

3 Add in the rosemary and mushrooms, season with salt and pepper and continue to cook for 2 minutes.

4 Pour in the wine and cook for a further minute to allow the alcohol to evaporate.

5 Pour in the cream, mix everything together and cook for 1 minute. Set aside.

6 Meanwhile cook the pasta in a large saucepan of boiling salted water until al dente. Drain and tip back into the same pan.

7 Pour in the cream sauce and toss everything together for 30 seconds to allow the flavours to combine.

8 Serve immediately.

TAGLIATELLE CON CARCIOFI E PROSCIUTTO CRUDO

Tagliatelle with artichokes and Parma ham

Everybody knows that I absolutely love artichokes. I wanted them to feature in at least two or three recipes so you could try them at their best. The inspiration for this dish came from me cutting artichokes in quarters and wrapping them in Parma ham for antipasti. From this I realised that it would be a perfect base to create one of the best recipes in this book. The colours are fantastic and the taste is even better.

Serves 4

6 tablespoons olive oil
2 red onions, peeled and finely sliced
10 slices of Parma ham, cut into strips across the width
10 artichokes hearts in oil, drained and quartered
100ml dry white wine
3 tablespoons freshly chopped flat leaf parsley
400g fresh egg tagliatelle, see page 21
80g piece of Parmesan cheese
salt and pepper to taste

1 Heat the oil in a large frying pan over a medium heat and fry the onions and Parma ham for 5 minutes, stirring occasionally with a wooden spoon.

2 Add the artichokes, season with salt and pepper and continue to cook for a further 3 minutes, stirring occasionally.

3 Pour in the wine and continue to cook for a further minute to allow the alcohol to evaporate. Sprinkle over the parsley, stir everything together and set aside.

4 Meanwhile cook the pasta in a large saucepan of boiling salted water until al dente. Drain and tip back into the same pan.

5 Pour in the sauce, return the saucepan to a low heat and toss everything together for 30 seconds to allow the flavours to combine.

6 Divide the pasta between four serving plates, scatter over shavings of Parmesan cheese and serve immediately.

DRIED PASTA

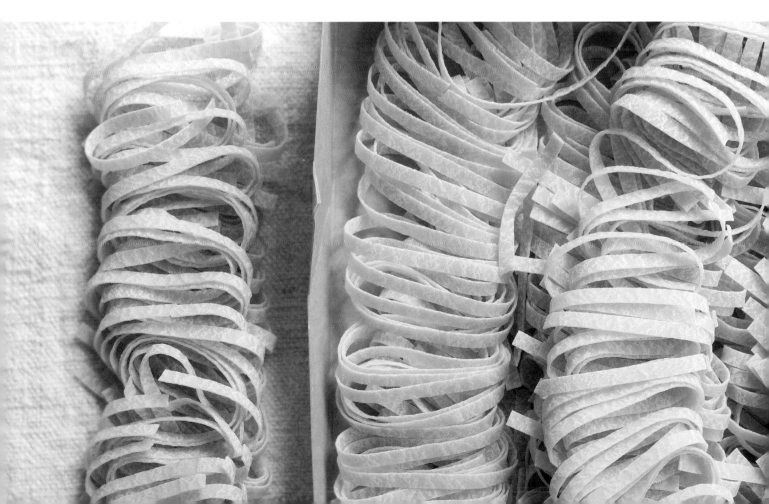

ORECCHIETTE AI BROCCOLI
Pasta shells with sprouting broccoli, chilli and pine nuts

My boys, Luciano and Rocco, absolutely love broccoli. It's by far their favourite vegetable and they would eat it every day if they could. I wanted to give them this dish (without the chilli) to see if they'd like it and honestly, I've never seen them eat so quickly. It was so great giving them an alternative option and I managed to introduce new flavours to them too. This is a really tasty recipe that anyone will love but if your children like broccoli it's a definite winner.

Serves 4

8 tablespoons olive oil
300g sprouting broccoli, cut into 2cm pieces
2 garlic cloves, finely sliced
6 tablespoons pine nuts
1 medium-hot red chilli, deseeded and finely sliced
100ml dry white wine
500g orecchiette shells
150g freshly grated Parmesan cheese
10 fresh purple basil leaves
salt to taste

1 Heat the oil in a large frying pan or wok over a medium heat and stir-fry the broccoli with the garlic, pine nuts and the chilli for 3 minutes, stirring occasionally with a wooden spoon.

2 Season with salt, add the white wine and continue to cook over a medium heat for a further 8 minutes. Make sure that the broccoli stays al dente.

3 Meanwhile cook the pasta in a large saucepan of boiling salted water until al dente. Drain and tip back into the same pan.

4 Add the broccoli mix to the pan with the pasta and place the pan over a low heat.

5 Sprinkle over the Parmesan cheese and mix everything together for 20 seconds to allow the sauce to coat the pasta evenly.

6 Serve immediately, garnished with the basil leaves.

LINGUINE AL TONNO

Linguine with tinned tuna, olives and chilli

Without doubt this has to be one of my father's favourite pasta dishes. I remember when I used to live with him it was a must-have dish at least once a week but not always with the same shape of pasta. Please make sure that you never use tuna in brine for this recipe and if you like you can add some capers to the sauce.

Serves 4
10 tablespoons extra virgin olive oil
2 garlic cloves, peeled and finely sliced
100g pitted Kalamata olives, drained and quartered
5 anchovy fillets in oil, drained and chopped
10 cherry tomatoes, quartered
$^1\!/_2$ teaspoon dried chilli flakes
1 x 200g tin tuna in oil, drained and flaked
2 tablespoons freshly chopped flat leaf parsley
500g linguine of your choice
salt to taste

1 Heat the oil in a large frying pan over a medium heat and fry the garlic, olives and anchovies for 1 minute, stirring with a wooden spoon.

2 Add in the tomatoes with the chilli and continue to cook for a further 2 minutes.

3 Scatter in the tuna with the parsley, season with a little salt and mix together for 1 minute. Set aside.

4 Meanwhile cook the pasta in a large saucepan of boiling salted water until al dente. Drain and tip back into the same pan over a low heat.

5 Pour in the tuna, tomato and olive sauce and stir everything together for 30 seconds to allow the flavours to combine.

6 Serve hot and please do not be tempted to serve it with grated cheese on top.

FUSILLI CON PEPERONI E ZUCCHINE
Fusilli with red peppers and courgettes

If you need a quick and impressive recipe with not a lot of washing up to do, this is the one to try. A great pasta dish for a romantic dinner because it's colourful, light and tasty. The combination of the courgettes, peppers and walnuts is divine and of course, it will all come together with the fresh lemon zest. Perfect for summer barbecues.

Serves 4
2 red peppers
2 courgettes
5 tablespoons olive oil
pinch of dried chilli flakes
4 tablespoons chopped walnuts
500g fusilli
zest of 1 unwaxed lemon
4 tablespoons freshly grated Pecorino cheese
salt to taste

1 Cut the peppers in half lengthways. Discard the stalk and seeds. Cut into thin slices and then chop into 0.5cm cubes.

2 Coarsely grate the courgettes in the middle of a clean tea towel and squeeze dry.

3 Heat the oil in a large frying pan over a medium heat and fry the peppers for 3 minutes, stirring occasionally with a wooden spoon.

4 Add in the courgettes, the chilli flakes and the nuts and continue to cook for a further 3 minutes. Season with salt and continue to stir occasionally.

5 Meanwhile cook the pasta in a large saucepan of boiling salted water until al dente. Drain and tip into the frying pan with the sauce.

6 Sprinkle over the lemon zest and stir everything together over a medium heat for 30 seconds to allow the flavours to combine.

7 Divide between four serving bowls and serve immediately topped with the Pecorino cheese.

RIGATONI AI CARCIOFI
Rigatoni with artichokes, garlic and orange zest

I have always found artichokes a little bit like Marmite.... you love them or you hate them! In my case, I absolutely adore them. If you have never tried them, please have a go at this pasta dish – you won't be disappointed. Never ever buy artichokes that are preserved in brine, they are not worth eating.

Serves 4

30g salted butter
6 tablespoons olive oil
2 garlic cloves, peeled and finely chopped
2 tablespoons finely chopped fresh rosemary
100g pitted Kalamata olives, halved
6 artichoke hearts in oil, drained and cut into quarters
100ml dry white wine
zest of ½ orange
500g rigatoni
salt and pepper to taste

1 Melt the butter with the oil in a large frying pan or a wok. Once hot add in the garlic, rosemary, olives and artichokes and cook over a medium heat for 3 minutes, stirring occasionally with a wooden spoon.

2 Pour in the wine and cook for a further 2 minutes to allow the alcohol to evaporate.

3 Add the orange zest, season with salt and pepper and mix everything together. Set aside.

4 Meanwhile cook the pasta in a large saucepan of boiling salted water until al dente. Drain and tip into the pan with the artichoke mixture.

5 Return the pan to a high heat and mix everything together for 30 seconds to allow the sauce to coat the pasta evenly.

6 Serve immediately.

SPAGHETTINI ALL'ARAGOSTA
Spaghettini with lobster and white wine

Often people ask me if I had to choose my last supper what would it be...Well, here it is. I know that lobster can be a little expensive but the flavour goes a long way and for a special occasion it really makes for a perfect plate of pasta. Substitute the spaghettini with linguine if you want but please never grate any kind of cheese on top of this dish.

Serves 2

1 whole live lobster, or a ready-cooked one if you prefer,
  weighing about 1kg
4 tablespoons extra virgin olive oil
1 garlic clove, peeled and finely sliced
1 small medium-hot red chilli, deseeded and finely sliced
1/2 glass of dry white wine
1 tablespoon freshly chopped flat leaf parsley
1 x 400g tin cherry tomatoes, only use half
250g spaghettini
salt to taste

1 To cook the live lobster, bring a large saucepan of water to the boil and cook the lobster for 10 minutes. Drain and leave to cool.

2 Twist off the claws and pincers and place on a chopping board. Using the back of a large heavy knife, crack open the large claws. Use a skewer to carefully remove all the meat from the claws and cut into chunks.

3 Place the lobster, back uppermost, on a chopping board and cut in half lengthways. Remove the meat from the body and cut into chunks. Clean the shell halves under cold running water and set aside.

4 Heat the oil in a large frying pan over a low heat and fry the garlic and chilli for about 30 seconds. Add in the lobster meat and cook for about 1 minute, stirring with a wooden spoon.

5 Pour in the white wine, scatter in the parsley and cook for a further minute to allow the alcohol to evaporate.

6 Add in the tomatoes, season with salt and continue to cook, uncovered, for 3 minutes, stirring occasionally. Set aside.

7 Meanwhile cook the pasta in a large saucepan of boiling salted water until al dente. Drain and tip back into the same pan.

8 Place the saucepan on a low heat and pour in the lobster sauce. Mix everything together for 30 seconds to allow the pasta to absorb the flavours of the lobster sauce.

9 To serve, spoon the pasta into the reserved lobster shells, pour over any remaining sauce and enjoy.

LINGUINE AL PESTO GENOVESE
Linguine with Genovese basil pesto

In the summer of 2008, I went to visit a friend of mine, Daniele, in the beautiful Ligurian region where basil grows at its best. He introduced me to pesto alla Genovese and I have to admit that since then it's been one of my top pasta recipes to cook at home. Please do not attempt to make pesto with dried basil because it will never work. If you prefer you can substitute the linguine with spaghetti.

Serves 4
50g fresh basil, leaves only
50g pine nuts
1 garlic clove, peeled
130ml extra virgin olive oil
25g freshly grated Parmesan cheese
500g linguine
salt and pepper to taste

1 Place the basil, pine nuts and garlic in a food processor. Drizzle in the oil and blitz until smooth.

2 Transfer the basil mixture into a large bowl and fold in the Parmesan cheese. Season with a little salt.

3 Cook the pasta in a large saucepan of boiling salted water until al dente. Drain and tip into the bowl with the pesto.

4 Toss everything together for 30 seconds to allow the pesto to coat the pasta evenly.

5 Serve immediately.

PENNE ALLA TREVISANA
Penne with red chicory, sausages and red wine

A pasta dish designed for a boys' night in watching football. This has great flavours, is very filling and, most importantly, is very simple to prepare. Make sure you buy good-quality pork sausages and you can substitute the penne with rigatoni if you wish.

Serves 4

150g good-quality pork sausages
3 tablespoons extra virgin olive oil
1 red onion, peeled and finely chopped
2 whole red chicory, washed and shredded
100ml red wine
500g penne rigate
30ml double cream
2 tablespoons freshly chopped flat leaf parsley
30g freshly grated Parmesan cheese
salt and pepper to taste

1 Remove the meat from the sausage skins.

2 Heat the oil in a large frying pan over a low heat and fry the sausage meat and onion for 5 minutes. Stir occasionally with a wooden spoon to allow the meat to crumble.

3 Add the chicory, season with salt and pepper and continue to cook for 1 minute.

4 Pour in the wine and continue to cook for a further minute to allow the alcohol to evaporate then set aside, away from the heat.

5 Meanwhile cook the pasta in a large saucepan of boiling salted water until al dente.

6 Once the pasta is ready, return the sauce to a medium heat. Drain the pasta and tip into the frying pan with the sauce.

7 Pour in the cream with the parsley, sprinkle with the Parmesan cheese then toss everything together over a medium heat for 30 seconds to allow the flavours to combine.

8 Serve immediately.

LINGUINE DI MARE
Seafood linguine with chilli and white wine

This is a recipe that you often find in Italian cookery books but mine will guarantee you minimum effort, maximum satisfaction. This pasta dish has all the flavours of the sea that you need but you won't find yourself in the kitchen cooking for hours. Please make sure that your seafood is fresh and if you fancy you can substitute the linguine with spaghetti.

Serves 4
250g clams
250g mussels
100ml dry white wine
6 tablespoons extra virgin olive oil
4 garlic cloves, peeled and sliced
$1/2$ teaspoon dried chilli flakes
2 x 400g tins cherry tomatoes
250g baby squid, quartered
250g uncooked prawns, peeled
4 tablespoons freshly chopped flat leaf parsley
500g linguine
zest of 1 unwaxed lemon
salt to taste

1 Wash the clams and mussels under cold water, discard any broken ones and those that do not close when tapped firmly.

2 Place in a large saucepan, pour in the wine, cover with the lid, and cook over a medium heat for 3 minutes until the shells have opened. Discard any shellfish that remain closed and tip the rest into a colander placed over a bowl to catch the cooking liquor. Set aside.

3 Heat the oil in the same saucepan that you used for the clams and mussels and gently fry the garlic until it begins to sizzle. Add the chilli and the tomatoes and cook over a medium heat for 5 minutes. Season with salt and stir occasionally.

4 Pour 6 tablespoons of the reserved cooking liquor from the shellfish into the sauce and continue to simmer for 2 minutes.

5 Stir in the baby squid and the prawns and continue to cook for a further 3 minutes until they turn pink.

6 Add the clams, mussels and the parsley and stir until heated through.

7 Meanwhile cook the pasta in a large saucepan of boiling salted water until al dente. Drain and tip into the pan with the sauce.

8 Sprinkle with the lemon zest and mix everything together over a low heat for 1 minute to allow the sauce to coat the pasta evenly.

9 Serve immediately.

FUSILLI AI FUNGHI E PORRI
Fusilli with chestnut mushrooms, leeks and mascarpone cheese

I must admit that this was one of my experiments that I tried one day. I knew that the combination of mushrooms, leeks and garlic would work beautifully and that the mascarpone, and chives would work, but all together? It was a gamble but a gamble that hit the jackpot. The combination is amazing – you are left with a creamy mushroom sauce but with different flavours peeking through with every bite and it really won't disappoint. You can substitute the fusilli with penne pasta if you fancy.

Serves 4
45g salted butter
250g chestnut mushrooms, sliced
2 leeks, washed and sliced 0.5cm thick
2 garlic cloves, peeled and finely chopped
250g mascarpone cheese
3 tablespoons freshly chopped chives
4 pinches cayenne pepper
500g fusilli
60g freshly grated Parmesan cheese
salt to taste

1 Melt the butter in a large frying pan over a medium heat. Add the mushrooms, leeks and garlic and fry for 5 minutes, stirring occasionally with a wooden spoon.

2 Spoon in the mascarpone and continue to cook for a further minute, stirring continuously. Stir in the chives and cayenne pepper, season with salt and remove from the heat.

3 Meanwhile cook the pasta in a large saucepan of boiling salted water until al dente. Drain and tip back into the same pan.

4 Pour in the mushroom sauce and stir everything together for 30 seconds to allow the flavours to combine.

5 Divide between four serving plates, sprinkle over the Parmesan cheese and serve immediately.

PIAZZA
DEL NETTUNO

SPAGHETTINI CON CAPESANTE IN SALSA VERDE
Spaghettini with scallops and parsley pesto

Scallops, parsley and garlic is a combination made in heaven. This very simple sauce had to be part of my pasta cookbook. This recipe is quick, colourful and will shout freshness every time you make it. Please don't buy frozen scallops and never choose curly parsley over the flat leaf variety. *Buon Appetito!*

Serves 4

45g salted butter
250g small scallops, without the coral
50g fresh flat leaf parsley, leaves only
50g pine nuts
2 tablespoons salted capers, rinsed under cold water
1 garlic clove, peeled
130ml extra virgin olive oil
zest of 1 unwaxed lemon
500g spaghettini
salt and pepper to taste

1 Melt the butter in a frying pan and cook the scallops for 1 minute on each side (you might want to do this in batches). Set aside.

2 Place the parsley, pine nuts, capers and garlic in a food processor. Drizzle in the oil and blitz until smooth.

3 Transfer the parsley mixture into a large bowl and mix in the scallops with the lemon zest. Season with salt and pepper.

4 Meanwhile cook the pasta in a large saucepan of boiling salted water until al dente. Drain and tip into the bowl with the pesto and scallops.

5 Gently toss everything together for 30 seconds allowing the pesto to coat the pasta evenly.

6 Serve immediately.

ORECCHIETTE CON CALAMARI E CHORIZO
Pasta shells and beans with squid and chorizo

I absolutely love squid and to me there is no better way to cook it than with a nice spicy chorizo sausage. This is a pasta dish that would be perfect for a party because the flavours and the colours are just amazing. If you prefer you can substitute the parsley leaves with fresh mint but whatever you do, please make sure that you use fresh squid.

Serves 6

100g tinned chick peas, drained
100g tinned borlotti beans, drained
15 cherry tomatoes, quartered
1 medium-hot red chilli, deseeded and thinly sliced
1 garlic clove, peeled and finely chopped
3 tablespoons freshly chopped flat leaf parsley
2 tablespoons freshly squeezed lemon juice
8 tablespoons extra virgin olive oil
400g squid (look for medium size ones)
80g hot chorizo sausage, thinly sliced
500g orecchiette shells
salt to taste

1 Put the chickpeas and beans in a large bowl with the tomatoes, chilli, garlic and parsley. Pour in the lemon juice and 5 tablespoons of the oil, season with salt and toss gently together. Set aside.

2 Cut open the body pouch of each squid along one side and use the tip of a small sharp knife to score the inner side into a fine diamond pattern. Then cut each pouch first in half lengthways and then across into 7cm pieces.

3 Heat the remaining oil in a large frying pan over a high heat and add in the squid pieces (scored side up so that they will curl attractively). Also add in the tentacles.

4 Sear for about 30 seconds, then turn them over and continue to sear for another 30 seconds until golden and caramelised. Season with salt, add the chorizo to the pan and cook for a further minute, keeping the heat high. Set aside.

5 Cook the pasta in a large saucepan of boiling salted water until al dente. Drain and tip back into the same pan.

6 Return the saucepan to a low heat and pour in the bean mixture, the squid and the chorizo. Stir everything together for 1 minute to allow the flavours to combine.

7 Serve immediately and please do not be tempted to serve it with any grated cheese on top.

LINGUINE AVELLINESI

Linguine with smoked salmon and spicy red pepper sauce

I learnt this recipe from a restaurant situated in the mountains of Avellino in the south of Italy. I remember that I was very impressed by the combination of the smoked salmon with the peppers, so I have decided to share it with all of you. I have also tried this pasta dish with smoked trout and to be honest it's just as good. Substitute linguine with fettuccine if you prefer and please make sure that you use a good-quality white wine.

Serves 4

30g salted butter
8 tablespoons olive oil
1 leek, washed and cut into 0.5cm slices
1 red pepper, halved, deseeded and diced into 0.5cm cubes
200g smoked salmon, cut into 0.5cm strips
1/2 teaspoon dried chilli flakes
60ml dry white wine
500g linguine
2 tablespoons freshly chopped flat leaf parsley
zest of 1 unwaxed lemon
salt to taste

1 Melt the butter with the oil in a large frying pan over a medium heat and fry the leek and pepper for 5 minutes, stirring occasionally with a wooden spoon.

2 Add the salmon and the chilli and continue to cook for 1 minute. Pour in the wine and cook for a further minute to allow the alcohol to evaporate. Season with a little salt and set aside.

3 Meanwhile cook the pasta in a large saucepan of boiling salted water until al dente. Drain and tip back into the same pan.

4 Pour in the salmon and pepper sauce along with the parsley and lemon zest. Return to a low heat and stir everything together for 30 seconds to allow the flavours to combine.

5 Serve immediately.

PENNE ALL' EMILIANA
Penne with peas, pork, rosemary and white wine

This recipe comes from the region of Emilia Romagna where pasta dishes are taken very, very seriously. I was there once on holiday and as a souvenir I brought back this beautiful meal. Although I have suggested you use frozen peas, please use fresh ones if they are in season. If you can't find fresh rosemary leaves, don't worry, you can always use fresh thyme leaves instead.

Serves 4

4 tablespoons olive oil
50g salted butter
450g pork chops, without the bone, cut into 1cm cubes
1 large onion, peeled and finely chopped
1 tablespoon finely chopped fresh rosemary leaves
150ml white wine
1 tablespoon tomato purée
200ml warm water
150g frozen peas, defrosted
500g penne rigate
50g freshly grated Parmesan cheese
salt and pepper to taste

1 Heat the oil and butter in a large frying pan over a medium heat and fry the pork and onion for 5 minutes, stirring occasionally with a wooden spoon allowing the meat to colour on all sides.

2 Add the rosemary, season with salt and pepper and continue to cook for 1 minute.

3 Pour in the wine and cook for a further minute to allow the alcohol to evaporate.

4 Mix in the tomato purée with the warm water and cook over a low heat for 40 minutes, stirring occasionally.

5 Add the peas and cook for a further 10 minutes then set aside, away from the heat.

6 Meanwhile cook the pasta in a large saucepan of boiling salted water until al dente. Drain and tip back into the same pan.

7 Pour in the sauce and stir everything together over a low heat for 30 seconds to allow the flavours to combine.

8 Serve immediately, sprinkled with Parmesan cheese.

LINGUINE ALLO ZAFFERANO
Linguine served with a delicate saffron sauce

For me, although this recipe has basic ingredients, it is offering someone something really special. It just oozes flavour and the saffron makes it that little more extravagant. It's like a mixture of an Italian and English carbonara with a twist and it works fantastically. You can substitute the linguine with tagliatelle or spaghetti and the ham with bacon if you prefer, but please leave in the saffron – it really makes the dish.

Serves 4
30g salted butter
150g cooked ham, cut into thin strips
pinch of saffron threads
250ml double cream
500g linguine
3 egg yolks
60g freshly grated Pecorino cheese
salt and pepper to taste

1 Melt the butter in a small frying pan and gently fry the ham for 2 minutes. Set aside.

2 Place the saffron in a medium saucepan with 4 tablespoons water. Bring to the boil then remove from the heat and let it rest for 5 minutes.

3 Pour the cream into the saucepan with the saffron and return the saucepan to the heat. Add in the ham and gently simmer for 3 minutes. Season with salt and pepper and set aside.

4 Meanwhile cook the pasta in a large saucepan of boiling salted water until al dente. Drain and tip into the pan with the saffron sauce.

5 Return the pan to a low heat and add the egg yolks, stirring continuously for 10 seconds so they cook in the residual heat.

6 Divide the linguine between four serving plates and serve immediately topped with grated Pecorino cheese.

SPAGHETTI POVERACCIO
Spaghetti with anchovies, breadcrumbs and garlic

The word povera means 'a poor man' and this is a recipe that was originally created to feed a lot of people with little money, allowing them to make use of inexpensive ingredients. Do not use anchovies marinated in vinegar because they won't work in this dish but by all means substitute the fresh chilli with dried chilli flakes. Please, please, please make sure that the pasta is cooked al dente.

Serves 4
6 tablespoons olive oil
3 garlic cloves, peeled and halved
8 anchovy fillets in oil, drained and chopped
1 medium-hot red chilli, deseeded and chopped
100g fresh white breadcrumbs
500g spaghetti
3 tablespoons freshly chopped flat leaf parsley
salt to taste

1 Heat the oil in a frying pan over a low heat and gently fry the garlic until golden all over. Remove the garlic and add the anchovies and chilli to the oil. Cook for about 3 minutes or until the anchovies have melted into the oil. Set aside.

2 In another frying pan, toast the breadcrumbs until crispy and golden brown. Set aside.

3 Cook the pasta in a large saucepan of boiling salted water until al dente. Drain and tip back into the pan over a low heat.

4 Pour in the anchovy oil, add the parsley and the breadcrumbs and stir everything together for 30 seconds to allow the flavours to combine.

5 Serve immediately.

RIGATONI CON ASPARAGI, PISELLI E FUNGHI

Rigatoni with peas and porcini mushroooms in a creamy asparagus sauce

For anybody who isn't a big fan of rich tomato sauces this has to be the perfect pasta recipe if you still want bags of flavour on your plate. This dish is so full of fresh ingredients that even though it's in a creamy sauce it doesn't feel heavy. I must admit that every time I make this for a vegetarian they utterly love me – so it must be good.

Serves 4

400g asparagus
50g salted butter
200g frozen peas, defrosted
30g dried porcini mushrooms, soaked in warm water for 15 minutes and drained
2 leeks, washed and cut into 0.5cm slices
200ml double cream
3 tablespoons freshly chopped flat leaf parsley
2 pinches of smoked paprika
500g rigatoni
60g freshly grated Pecorino cheese
salt to taste

1 Use a potato peeler to scrape the asparagus stalks, discarding the woody ends. Chop the stalks into 2cm long pieces. Drop into a medium saucepan of boiling salted water and cook for 2 minutes. Drain and immediately refresh under cold running water to prevent them from discolouring. Set aside.

2 Melt the butter in a large frying pan over a medium heat. Add the peas, mushrooms, leeks and asparagus and fry for 5 minutes, stirring occasionally with a wooden spoon.

3 Pour in the cream and continue to cook for a further minute, stirring continuously.

4 Mix in the parsley and paprika, season with salt and set aside.

5 Meanwhile cook the pasta in a large saucepan of boiling salted water until al dente. Drain and tip back into the same pan.

6 Pour in the asparagus sauce and stir everything together for 30 seconds to allow the flavours to combine.

7 Divide between four serving plates, sprinkle over the Pecorino cheese and serve immediately.

SPAGHETTI CON PEPERONI ALLE ERBE
Spaghetti with yellow peppers, chilli and herbs

If I was a vegetarian, this is the kind of dish that I would eat regularly. I absolutely love peppers, especially when you add such fabulous herbs to them. You would think that the flavours would overpower each other with three different herbs, chilli and garlic, but I promise you it is a combination that really gets those tastebuds working. You can also use aubergines instead of peppers If you like.

Serves 4
8 tablespoons olive oil
2 garlic cloves, peeled and finely sliced
4 yellow peppers, deseeded and finely sliced
1 teaspoon dried chilli flakes
1 teaspoon fresh thyme leaves
1 tablespoon finely chopped fresh rosemary leaves
2 tablespoons finely chopped fresh flat leaf parsley
500g spaghetti
salt to taste

1 Heat the oil in a large frying pan over a low heat and gently fry the garlic and peppers for 2 minutes.

2 Add the chilli with all the herbs and continue to cook for a further 6 minutes, stirring occasionally with a wooden spoon. Season with salt and set aside, away from the heat.

3 Meanwhile cook the pasta in a large saucepan of boiling salted water until al dente. Drain and tip back into the same pan.

4 Pour in the pepper mixture and stir everything together over a low heat for 30 seconds to allow the sauce to coat the pasta evenly.

5 Serve immediately.

BAKED & SWEET PASTA

CANNELLONI DEL NONNO

Cannelloni filled with rocket, spinach and ricotta cheese

A great baked pasta dish that has been in my family for over twenty years. If you prefer, you can substitute the Pecorino cheese with Parmesan.

Serves 6–8

400g fresh egg pasta dough, see page 19
720ml passata (sieved tomatoes)
15 fresh basil leaves
30g freshly grated Pecorino cheese

For the filling

500g ricotta cheese
150g frozen spinach, defrosted and squeezed to remove the excess water
150g rocket leaves, chopped
1/4 teaspoon freshly grated nutmeg
60g freshly grated Pecorino cheese
salt and pepper to taste

For the béchamel sauce

100g salted butter
100g plain flour
1 litre cold full-fat milk
1/4 teaspoon freshly grated nutmeg

1 Preheat the oven to 180°C/fan 160°C/gas mark 4.

2 Pour the passata into a large bowl with the basil leaves. Season with salt and pepper, mix together and set aside.

3 To prepare the béchamel sauce, melt the butter in a large saucepan over a medium heat. Stir in the flour and cook for 1 minute until it turns light brown in colour. Gradually whisk in the cold milk, reduce the heat and cook for 10 minutes, whisking constantly. Once thickened, stir in the nutmeg. Season with salt and pepper and set aside to cool slightly.

4 To prepare the filling, place all the ingredients in a large bowl, season with salt and pepper and use a fork to mix everything together. Leave in the fridge to rest while you prepare the pasta.

5 Flatten the prepared dough with your fingers so that it can fit through the rollers of the pasta machine. Flour the pasta lightly on both sides and start to roll it from the widest setting to the thinnest. Cut it into rectangles measuring 7 x 15cm – you will need 26 sheets of pasta.

6 Prepare a large saucepan with plenty of boiling salted water and start to cook the pasta sheets – work in batches of five. Boil the sheets for 1 minute then remove and place immediately in a large bowl of cold water to prevent the pasta going soggy. After 1 minute in the cold water, remove the sheets of pasta and place on a clean tea towel.

7 Place 1 1/2 tablespoons of filling across each pasta sheet and start to roll up the pasta from the narrow side going forward. To seal the cannelloni, overlap the pasta sheet by about 2cm. Repeat until all the pasta sheets are filled.

8 Select a rectangular dish measuring 25 x 35cm and pour in a third of the béchamel sauce. Spread evenly. Place half of the cannelloni onto the béchamel layer with the seam facing down. Spoon over half of the passata and half of the remaining béchamel sauce.

9 Build up the second layer of cannelloni and spoon over the remaining passata. Spread over the remaining béchamel sauce. Finish by sprinkling over the Pecorino cheese and bake in the centre of the oven for 35 minutes or until coloured and crispy.

10 Once ready, leave it to rest for 5 minutes out of the oven. It will be easier to cut and serve as the layers will hold together.

FARFALLE AL SALMONE GRATINATE
Crispy topped farfalle with smoked salmon and chives

If you like smoked salmon and creamy sauces, this recipe will really rock your world. An elegant yet full of flavour dish that's got the wow factor. You can use medium size shells instead of the bow pasta but please make sure that you get your béchamel sauce right; it should not be too runny.

Serves 6
350g farfalle
80g salted butter, plus extra for greasing
200g smoked salmon, cut into small strips
3 tablespoons finely chopped fresh chives
100g freshly grated Parmesan cheese
salt and pepper to taste

For the béchamel sauce
50g salted butter
50g plain flour
500ml cold full-fat milk
1/2 teaspoon paprika
pinch of freshly grated nutmeg

1 First make the béchamel sauce. Melt the butter in a large saucepan over a medium heat. Stir in the flour and cook for 1 minute until it turns light brown in colour. Gradually whisk in the cold milk, reduce the heat and cook for 10 minutes, whisking constantly. Once thickened, stir in the paprika and the nutmeg. Season with salt and pepper and set aside to cool slightly.

2 Meanwhile cook the pasta in a large saucepan of boiling salted water until al dente. Drain and place in a large bowl with the butter, smoked salmon, chives, half the Parmesan and half the béchamel sauce. Mix everything together.

3 Preheat the grill to medium-high. Grease a 22cm round ovenproof dish with sides at least 4cm deep. Pour the pasta into the dish, cover with the remaining béchamel sauce and sprinkle over the remaining Parmesan cheese.

4 Place the dish under the preheated grill and cook for 15 minutes until golden and crispy.

5 Once ready, leave it to rest for 5 minutes. It will be easier to cut and serve as the layers will hold together.

GNOCCHI AL POMODORO
Potato dumplings with tomato sauce and Cheddar cheese

When I first met my wife she told me that one of her favourite Italian dishes was Gnocchi al pomodoro. Her mother, Elizabeth, used to make it for her when she was a little girl and they lived in Italy and every time I make this recipe I can still see those distant memories in her eyes. It is a really homely dish that all the family will love. You can substitute the Cheddar for Parmesan cheese if you prefer and please make sure you don't overcook the gnocchi or they'll go soggy.

Serves 4
4 tablespoons extra virgin olive oil
1 large red onion, peeled and finely chopped
700ml passata (sieved tomatoes)
10 fresh basil leaves
500g ready-made plain gnocchi
100g freshly grated mature Cheddar cheese
salt and pepper to taste

1 Preheat the oven to 200°C/fan 180°C/gas mark 6.

2 Heat the oil in a medium saucepan and fry the onion over a medium heat for about 3 minutes until golden. Pour in the passata and cook for 10 minutes, stirring occasionally with a wooden spoon.

3 Stir in the basil, season with salt and pepper and set aside, away from the heat.

4 Meanwhile, half-fill a medium saucepan with water, add 1 tablespoon of salt and bring to the boil.

5 Cook the gnocchi in the boiling water removing them as soon as they start to float to the top. Drain and place in the saucepan with the sauce. Gently stir everything together to allow the sauce to coat the gnocchi evenly.

6 Transfer to a baking dish. Scatter over the Cheddar cheese and bake in the middle of the oven for 8 minutes until golden and bubbling.

7 Serve immediately.

CONCHIGLIE DI MARE
Shell pasta with prawns and saffron

Most of my food memories growing up in Naples consist of seafood. We ate it almost every day because we lived by the coast. Coming to England I realised that many people prefer creamy sauces, so quite often I take traditional recipes and add a little twist for the British palate. Please buy fresh prawns and make sure you only use flat leaf parsley and not the curly variety.

Serves 6
350g medium shell pasta (look for conchiglie)
80g salted butter, plus extra for greasing
300g fresh prawns, peeled (with head and tail removed)
100g fresh baby leaf spinach, washed
4 tablespoons finely chopped fresh flat leaf parsley
100g freshly grated Grana Padano cheese
salt and pepper to taste

For the béchamel sauce
50g salted butter
50g plain flour
500ml cold full-fat milk
4 x 0.125g sachets saffron powder
pinch of freshly grated nutmeg

1 To prepare the béchamel sauce, melt the butter in a large saucepan over a medium heat. Stir in the flour and cook for 1 minute until it turns light brown in colour. Gradually whisk in the cold milk, reduce the heat and cook for 10 minutes, whisking constantly. Once thickened, stir in the saffron and nutmeg. Season with salt and pepper and set aside to cool slightly.

2 Meanwhile cook the pasta in a large saucepan of boiling salted water until al dente. Drain and place in a large bowl with the butter, the prawns, spinach, parsley, half of the Grana Padano cheese and half of the béchamel sauce. Mix everything together to allow the ingredients to coat the pasta evenly. Preheat the grill to medium-high.

3 Grease a 22cm round ovenproof dish with sides at least 4cm deep. Pour the pasta into the dish and level the surface. Cover with the remaining béchamel sauce and sprinkle over the remaining Grana Padano cheese.

4 Place the dish under the preheated grill and cook for 15 minutes until golden and crispy.

5 Once ready, allow it to rest for 5 minutes. It will be easier to cut and serve as the layers will hold together.

GRANA PADANO
€ 16,50
1L KG

MACCHERONI GRATINATI
Baked pasta with ham and cheese

This is the kind of dish that ticks all the right boxes. You have the crispness of cheesy topping and the sumptuous cheese flavours with the saltiness of the ham and the sweetness of the peas. You won't need a massive portion of this pasta as it is very heavy, but it is so tasty that you won't be disappointed. What's really great about this recipe is that you can make it in the morning, cover with foil and refrigerate it ready to cook in the evening. You can substitute the Pecorino cheese with Parmesan if you prefer. Perfect served with a glass of cold beer.

Serves 4
15g salted butter
300g cooked ham, cut into 0.5cm cubes
300g maccheroni or penne
250ml double cream
100g freshly grated Red Leicester cheese
100g freshly grated mature Cheddar cheese
100g Gorgonzola cheese, cut into small chunks
1/4 teaspoon freshly grated nutmeg
2 mozzarella balls, drained and cut into 1cm cubes
3 egg yolks
150g frozen peas, defrosted
100g freshly grated Pecorino cheese
salt and pepper to taste

1 Preheat the oven to 220°C/fan 200°C/gas mark 7.

2 Melt the butter in a frying pan and fry the ham for 3 minutes until crispy. Set aside.

3 Meanwhile cook the pasta in a large saucepan of boiling salted water until al dente. Drain and tip back into the saucepan, away from the heat.

4 Pour in the cream with the Red Leicester, Cheddar and Gorgonzola. Return the saucepan to a low heat and use a wooden spoon to start to mix everything together for 1 minute.

5 Remove the pan from the heat and add in the nutmeg, the mozzarella, the egg yolks, the peas, the ham and half of the Pecorino cheese. Season with a little salt, plenty of black pepper and stir together for 30 seconds.

6 Tip the pasta into a 30cm round shallow dish, sprinkle over the remaining Pecorino cheese and bake in the centre of the preheated oven for about 15 minutes or until it is bubbling and blistering on top.

7 Once ready, leave it to rest for 5 minutes out of the oven before cutting into portions.

CANNELLONI ALLA MARGHERITA
Cannelloni filled with sun-dried tomatoes,
mozzarella and basil

This dish was inspired by the famous pizza margherita –
basically tomato, mozzarella and basil – fresh ingredients,
great colours and bags of flavours.

Serves 6–8
400g fresh egg pasta dough, see page 19
720ml passata (sieved tomatoes)
15 fresh basil leaves
50g freshly grated Parmesan cheese
2 mozzarella balls, drained and finely sliced

For the filling
500g ricotta cheese
20g fresh basil leaves, chopped
200g sun-dried tomatoes in oil, drained
1/4 teaspoon freshly grated nutmeg
3 mozzarella balls, drained and cut into 1cm cubes
salt and pepper to taste

For the béchamel sauce
100g salted butter
100g plain flour
1 litre cold full-fat milk
1/4 teaspoon freshly grated nutmeg

1 Preheat the oven to 180°C/fan 160°C/gas mark 4.

2 First make the béchamel sauce following the method
described on page 84.

3 Pour the passata into a large bowl with the basil leaves.
Season with salt and pepper, mix together and set aside.

4 To prepare the filling, place all the ingredients, except
the mozzarella, in a large bowl, season and use a fork
to mix everything together. Scatter over the cubed
mozzarella, fold together and leave in the fridge to rest.

5 Flatten the prepared dough with your fingers so that
it can fit through the rollers of the pasta machine. Flour
the pasta lightly on both sides and start to roll it from
the widest setting to the thinnest. Cut into rectangles
measuring 7 x 15cm. You will need 26 sheets of pasta.

6 Prepare a large saucepan with plenty of boiling salted
water and start to cook the pasta sheets – work in batches
of five. Boil the sheets for 1 minute then remove and
place immediately in a large bowl of cold water to prevent
the pasta going soggy. After 1 minute in the cold water,
remove the sheets of pasta and place on a clean tea towel.

7 Place 1 1/2 tablespoons of filling across each pasta sheet
and start to roll up the pasta from the narrow side going
forward. To seal the cannelloni, overlap each pasta sheet
by about 2cm. Repeat until all the pasta sheets are filled.

8 Select a rectangular dish measuring 25 x 35cm and
pour in a third of the béchamel sauce. Spread evenly.
Place half of the cannelloni onto the béchamel layer with
the seam facing down. Spoon over half of the passata and
half of the remaining béchamel sauce.

9 Build up the second layer of cannelloni and spoon
over the remaining passata. Spread over the remaining
béchamel sauce. Finish by sprinkling over the Parmesan
cheese and bake in the middle of the oven for 20 minutes.

10 Remove the dish from the oven, place the slices of
mozzarella on top and continue to bake for a further
15 minutes until golden and crispy.

11 Once ready, leave it to rest for 5 minutes out of the
oven. It will be easier to cut and serve as the layers will
hold together.

CONCHIGLIONI RIPIENI AL FORNO
Large pasta shells filled with pork and rosemary

Often when you have a party, you look for dishes that you can prepare in advance and then cook at the last minute when your guests arrive. Well – you've just found one. Once you've stuffed the large pasta shells, the only thing left to do is to bake them at the last minute. Substitute the minced pork for lamb or beef if you fancy.

Serves 4

24 large pasta shells (look for conchiglioni)
5 tablespoons olive oil
1 onion, peeled and finely chopped
500g minced pork
1 tablespoon finely chopped fresh rosemary leaves
2 x 400g tins chopped tomatoes
15 fresh basil leaves
80g freshly grated Pecorino cheese
salt and pepper to taste

For the béchamel sauce
50g salted butter
50g plain flour
500ml cold full-fat milk
pinch of freshly grated nutmeg

1 Bring a large pan of salted water to the boil. Parboil the pasta for about 5 minutes then drain and place the shells, inverted, on a clean tea towel to cool.

2 To prepare the béchamel sauce, melt the butter in a large saucepan over a medium heat. Stir in the flour and cook for 1 minute until it turns light brown in colour. Gradually whisk in the cold milk, reduce the heat and cook for 10 minutes, whisking constantly. Once thickened, stir in the nutmeg. Season with salt and pepper and set aside to cool.

3 Heat the oil in a large frying pan over a medium heat and cook the onion for 2 minutes until golden.

4 Add in the pork mince with the rosemary and stir continuously with a wooden spoon to allow the meat to crumble. Cook for 15 minutes until the meat has browned. Set aside to cool. Preheat the oven to 180°C/fan 160°C/gas mark 4.

5 Once the pork has cooled, pour half of the béchamel sauce into the pan and mix together.

6 Pour the chopped tomatoes into a small saucepan and heat through. When bubbling, add the basil and season with salt and pepper. Cook for 5 minutes.

7 Spread the tomato sauce over the bottom of a 35 x 20cm ceramic dish; this will prevent the pasta shells from sticking.

8 Using a tablespoon, fill the pasta shells with the pork mixture and gently place in the ceramic dish, making sure the shells aren't too close together. Drizzle the remaining béchamel over each filled shell.

9 Cover with foil and bake in the middle of the oven for 15 minutes. Remove the foil, sprinkle with the Pecorino cheese and continue to cook for a further 5 minutes or until the cheese is golden.

10 Once ready, allow to rest out of the oven for 3 minutes.

11 To serve, spoon some tomato sauce in the centre of each plate and arrange six filled pasta shells on top.

PENNE CON ZUCCHINE E SALAME GRATINATE

Crispy topped pasta with courgettes and salami

I designed this recipe one morning when my wife kept mentioning that the food she was going to prepare for a family get-together was a little bit boring. She asked me to come up with something more exciting to serve everyone. The only problem was that unfortunately I did not prepare enough, so my only tip would be that if you try this recipe for a party make sure that you have plenty because your guests will love it. If you do have some left over, you can use it the day after for your lunchbox or a picnic.

Serves 6
6 tablespoons olive oil
2 large courgettes, cut into 0.5cm cubes
350g penne rigate
250g salami Milano, cut into small strips
3 tablespoons freshly chopped flat leaf parsley
100g freshly grated Parmesan cheese
butter, for greasing
salt and pepper to taste

For the béchamel sauce
50g salted butter
50g plain flour
500ml cold full-fat milk
1/2 teaspoon paprika
pinch of freshly grated nutmeg

1 Heat the oil in a large frying pan over a medium heat and fry the courgettes for 5 minutes, stirring occasionally. Season with salt and pepper then set aside.

2 To prepare the béchamel sauce, melt the butter in a large saucepan over a medium heat. Stir in the flour and cook for 1 minute until it turns light brown in colour. Gradually whisk in the cold milk, reduce the heat and cook for 10 minutes, whisking constantly. Once thickened, stir in the paprika and nutmeg. Season with salt and pepper and set aside to cool slightly.

3 Meanwhile cook the pasta in a large saucepan of boiling salted water until al dente. Drain and tip into a large bowl with the courgettes, salami, parsley, half of the Parmesan cheese and half of the béchamel sauce. Gently mix everything together.

4 Preheat the grill to medium-high. Butter a 22cm round ovenproof dish with sides at least 4cm deep. Pour the pasta into the dish, cover with the remaining béchamel sauce and sprinkle over the remaining Parmesan cheese.

5 Place the dish under the preheated grill and cook for 15 minutes until golden and crispy.

6 Once ready, leave it to rest for 5 minutes. It will be easier to cut and serve as the layers will hold together.

CANNELLONI TONNO E RICOTTA
Cannelloni filled with tuna, ricotta cheese and lemon

I love cannelloni but wanted to create a dish that was a little bit different from the traditional fillings offered in most cookbooks or restaurants. This filling is so fresh and tasty and yet it has to be the easiest to prepare by far. Only use tuna in oil and not brine and if you don't have very much time you can buy the fresh cannelloni tubes ready to be filled, but promise me that you will try and make your own at least once. It's the most satisfying thing in the world and not as hard as you might think.

Serves 4
300g fresh egg pasta dough, see page 19

For the filling
250g ricotta cheese
250g tinned tuna chunks in oil, drained
zest of 1/2 unwaxed lemon
2 tablespoons freshly chopped chives
salt and pepper to taste

For the béchamel sauce
30g salted butter
30g plain flour
300ml cold full-fat milk
1/4 teaspoon freshly grated nutmeg

1 Preheat the oven to 180°C/fan 160°C/gas mark 4.

2 To prepare the béchamel sauce, melt the butter in a large saucepan over a medium heat. Stir in the flour and cook for 1 minute until it turns light brown in colour. Gradually whisk in the cold milk, reduce the heat and cook for 10 minutes, whisking constantly. Once thickened, stir in the nutmeg. Season with salt and pepper and set aside to cool slightly.

3 To prepare the filling, place all the ingredients in a large bowl, season with salt and pepper and use a fork to mix everything together until smooth. Leave in the fridge to rest while you cook the pasta sheets.

4 Flatten the prepared dough with your fingers so that it can fit through the rollers of the pasta machine. Flour the pasta lightly on both sides and start to roll it from the widest setting to the thinnest. Make sure you keep the pasta dusted with flour at all times. Cut into rectangles measuring 7 x 15cm. You will need 16 sheets of pasta in total.

5 Prepare a large saucepan of boiling salted water. Start to cook the pasta sheets, working in batches of four. Boil the sheets for 1 minute then remove and place in a large bowl of cold water to prevent the pasta going soggy. After 1 minute in the cold water, remove the sheets of pasta and place onto a clean tea towel.

6 Place 1 1/2 tablespoons of filling on each pasta sheet and start to roll up the pasta from the narrow side. To seal the cannelloni, overlap each pasta sheet by about 2cm. Repeat until all the pasta sheets are filled.

7 Select a rectangular dish measuring about 25 x 35cm and pour in half of the béchamel sauce. Spread evenly over the base. Place the cannelloni onto the béchamel with the seam facing down. Spread the remaining béchamel sauce over the cannelloni.

8 Cover with foil and bake in the middle of the oven for 15 minutes. Remove the foil and continue to bake for a further 20 minutes.

9 Once ready, leave it to rest for 5 minutes out of the oven. It will be easier to cut and serve as the shapes will hold together.

TORTA DI SPAGHETTI E SPINACI
Spaghetti and spinach tart

I love tarts and considering that I also love pasta, for me there is nothing better than pasta in a tart. I can guarantee that you have never seen a recipe like this in any other cookery book and once you've tried it, there will be no going back. If you want, substitute the spinach with rocket and serve with a cold glass of dry white wine.

Serves 8
200g spaghetti
5 tablespoons olive oil
2 red onions, peeled and thinly sliced
400g ready-made shortcrust pastry
plain flour, for dusting
300g baby leaf spinach, washed and roughly chopped
6 medium eggs
100g freshly grated Parmesan cheese
salt and pepper to taste

1 Pour 2 litres of water in a large saucepan and bring to the boil with 1 tablespoon of salt. Cook the pasta in the boiling salted water until al dente. Drain the pasta through a colander and rinse under cold running water immediately, to stop the pasta cooking. Once cold leave on the side to drain for 5 minutes. Give the pasta a good shake every minute or so.

2 Preheat the oven to 180°C/fan 160°C/gas mark 4. Heat the olive oil in a large frying pan over a medium heat and cook the onions for 5–6 minutes, stirring occasionally, until softened. Set aside.

3 Roll out the pastry on a lightly floured surface and use to line a 25cm loose-based tart tin. Chill in the freezer for 10 minutes.

4 Fill the tart tin with baking paper and baking beans, place on a baking tray and cook in the middle of the oven for 15 minutes. Remove the paper and beans and set the tart case aside to cool.

5 Meanwhile blanch the spinach by placing it in a colander over the sink and pouring boiling water over it. Squeeze out the excess water and set aside.

6 Lightly beat the eggs in a large bowl. Add the cheese, onions, spinach and the pasta and season with salt and pepper. Mix everything together then tip into the pastry case, spreading the mixture out evenly.

7 Bake in the middle of the oven for about 30 minutes or until the filling is just set. Remove from the oven and allow the tart to cool in the tin for 15 minutes before removing the tin and transferring the tart to a serving plate.

8 Cut into slices and serve warm or at room temperature with your favourite salad.

TIMBALLO ALLA TORRESE
Baked pasta with meat sauce and Parmesan cheese

This beautiful pasta bake traditionally comes from the town where I was born, Torre del Greco, in the south of Italy. This is where mozzarella comes from and, of course, is used in many recipes. I've used minced beef and pork together because I really believe that it gives a better texture to the sauce and please make sure you also use a good red wine.

Serves 6
4 tablespoons olive oil
1 onion, peeled and finely chopped
1 large carrot, peeled and grated
2 celery sticks, finely chopped
500g minced beef
500g minced pork
2 glasses of dry red wine

700ml passata (sieved tomatoes)
2 tablespoons tomato purée
200ml chicken stock
500g fettuccine
45g salted butter
4 tablespoons toasted breadcrumbs
3 mozzarella balls, drained and sliced
 (do not use buffalo mozzarella)
80g freshly grated Parmesan cheese
salt and pepper to taste

1 Heat the olive oil in a large saucepan over a medium heat and cook the onion, carrot and celery for 5 minutes, stirring occasionally with a wooden spoon.

2 Add in the minced meats and continue to cook for a further 5 minutes, stirring continuously until coloured all over. Season with salt and pepper.

3 Pour in the wine, stir well and continue to cook for 5 minutes to allow the alcohol to evaporate.

4 Pour in the passata with the tomato purée and the stock, lower the heat and cook, uncovered, for 2 hours, stirring the sauce every 20 minutes.

5 Once the sauce is ready, remove from the heat, season to taste with salt and pepper and set aside.

6 Cook the pasta in a large saucepan of boiling salted water until al dente. Drain and tip back into the same pan. Pour in the meat sauce and gently stir everything together to allow the flavours to combine.

7 Preheat the oven to 180°C/fan 160°C/gas mark 4. Butter a 30cm gratin dish and sprinkle over the breadcrumbs.

8 Spoon half the pasta mixture into the dish and scatter over the mozzarella cheese. Cover with the remaining pasta.

9 Dot the surface with the remaining butter and sprinkle over the Parmesan cheese.

10 Bake in the middle of the oven for 20 minutes until it is bubbling and blistering on top.

11 Before serving, let it rest for 5 minutes out of the oven before cutting into portions.

FARFALLE AL CARTOCCIO
Pasta baked with peppers and mozzarella

This pasta dish has definitely got the wow factor. Great colours, a fantastic smell and, most importantly, flavours that are out of this world. Please do not use buffalo mozzarella because it will be too milky and therefore make the pasta soggy. If you prefer you can sprinkle Parmesan cheese over the top once the pasta is ready to be served.

Serves 4

400g farfalle
5 tablespoons extra virgin olive oil
1 yellow pepper, halved, deseeded and chopped
   into 1cm cubes
1 red pepper, halved, deseeded and chopped
   into 1cm cubes
1 garlic clove, peeled and finely sliced
1 unwaxed lemon
4 tablespoons freshly chopped flat leaf parsley
2 mozzarella balls, drained and cut into 1cm pieces
salt and pepper to taste

1 Preheat the oven to 200°C/fan 180°C/gas mark 6. Pour 4 litres of water in a large saucepan and bring to the boil with 2 tablespoons salt.

2 Cook the pasta in the boiling salted water until al dente. Drain the pasta through a colander and rinse under cold running water immediately, to stop the pasta cooking. Once cold leave on the side to drain for 5 minutes. Give the pasta a good shake every minute or so.

3 Heat the oil in a large frying pan and gently fry the peppers with the garlic for 5 minutes, stirring occasionally. Transfer the mixture to a large bowl and set aside to cool.

4 Squeeze over the juice of half the lemon and mix in the pasta and the parsley. Season with salt and pepper.

5 Prepare 4 sheets of foil, each measuring about 30 x 30cm.

6 Divide the pasta between the sheets of foil and scatter over the mozzarella. Create a sealed parcel by bringing in the edges and scrunching together. Place on a baking sheet and bake in the preheated oven for 15 minutes.

7 To serve, place the parcels on serving plates, open and enjoy immediately.

GNOCCHI ALLA ROMANA CON PROSCIUTTO
Semolina gnocchi with Parma ham

An authentic dish that comes from the region of Lazio and to be more precise, near the capital of Italy, Rome. It is well known that the Romans make gnocchi with semolina instead of potatoes and that they will only use Pecorino Romano rather than Parmesan cheese. To make the recipe easier to prepare you can use 'quick cook' semolina instead of the traditional variety, which will take you much longer to cook.

Serves 6
550ml full-fat milk
550ml water
1/4 teaspoon freshly grated nutmeg
300g coarse semolina flour
150g salted butter
200g freshly grated Pecorino Romano cheese
4 eggs, beaten
6 tablespoons olive oil
2 garlic cloves, peeled and thinly sliced
2 x 400g tins chopped tomatoes
10 fresh basil leaves
12 slices of Parma ham
salt and pepper to taste

1 Put the milk, water and nutmeg in a large saucepan and bring to the boil.

2 Sprinkle in the semolina with one hand so that it falls like rain into the pan, while whisking constantly to prevent lumps forming. Continue to whisk until the mixture begins to thicken. Change the whisk for a wooden spoon and continue to cook over a medium heat for about 10 minutes. The semolina is ready when the mixture begins to come away from the sides of the pan.

3 Remove from the heat and mix in a third of the butter, half of the cheese and the eggs. Season with salt and pepper.

4 Lightly dampen a clean work surface with a little cold water and, using a metal spatula, spread out the semolina until it is about 2cm thick. Allow to cool and harden. Meanwhile preheat the oven to 200°C/fan 180°C/gas mark 6.

5 Once the semolina has firmed up, use a 5cm pastry cutter to stamp out circles, reserving the scraps.

6 Use a little of the remaining butter to grease a shallow ovenproof serving dish approximately 35 x 20cm. Arrange a layer of scraps from the semolina circles on the base of the dish. Lay the semolina circles on top, slightly overlapping.

7 Sprinkle the remaining cheese on top, cut the remaining butter into little knobs and scatter over the gnocchi. Sprinkle with black pepper and cook in the middle of the oven for 30 minutes.

8 Meanwhile heat the olive oil in a large saucepan over a medium heat and fry the garlic for 30 seconds. Add the chopped tomatoes and basil and season with salt and pepper. Allow to simmer, uncovered, for 15 minutes, stirring occasionally.

9 Once the gnocchi are ready, pour the tomato sauce in the middle of a serving dish, scoop over the gnocchi and serve immediately with the Parma ham twisted on top.

PENNE E PEPERONATA AL FORNO
Penne with roasted peppers and mozzarella

However much effort you put into a vegetarian meal, sometimes, although tasty, it can still be a little boring. This dish has the lot and offers that special person something a bit more creative. The saltiness of the capers and olives combined with the freshness of the parsley and the creaminess of the mozzarella is a winner every time. It's a really hearty meal and will satisfy everyone – even meat lovers. *Buon Appetito!*

Serves 4

3 tablespoons olive oil
1 garlic clove, peeled and finely sliced
600g roasted peppers (from a tin or jar), drained and sliced
1 tablespoon salted capers, rinsed
100g pitted Kalamata olives
320g penne rigate
1 tablespoon freshly chopped flat leaf parsley
2 mozzarella balls, drained and sliced
salt and pepper to taste

1 Heat the olive oil in a medium saucepan and gently fry the garlic until golden, then add the peppers, capers and olives. Season with salt and pepper, stir and simmer over a medium heat for about 10 minutes, stirring occasionally.

2 Meanwhile cook the pasta in a large saucepan of boiling salted water until al dente. Drain and tip into the saucepan with the peppers. Sprinkle over the parsley and mix together.

3 Preheat the grill to high.

4 Place the pasta in an ovenproof dish measuring about 30 x 15cm and cover the surface with the sliced mozzarella.

5 Grind over some black pepper and place under the preheated grill for 5 minutes or until the cheese is golden and melted.

6 Serve hot.

MEZZELUNE DOLCI
Half-moon shaped sweet pasta filled with candied fruit

This is a classic Neapolitan dessert that is usually eaten around Easter time. I remember like it was yesterday, my grandmother filling the pasta with candied fruits and ricotta cheese and me trying to help her as much as I could – because I knew I'd get an extra portion at the end. You can use good-quality chocolate chips instead of candied fruit.

Serves 6–8
For the sweet pasta
3 whole eggs and 2 extra yolks
300g plain flour, plus extra for dusting
50g butter, softened
4 tablespoons Amaretto liqueur
1 litre vegetable oil (for deep frying)
icing sugar, for dusting

For the filling
40g caster sugar
250g ricotta cheese
zest of 1 orange, finely chopped
10 almonds, finely chopped
40g candied fruit, finely chopped

1 Beat 2 of the eggs in a bowl and set aside.

2 To make the sweet pasta dough, place the remaining 1 egg and 2 egg yolks in a food processor. Add the flour, butter and Amaretto and mix together. Turn out the mixture onto a well-floured surface and knead for 2 minutes until you have a soft dough. Cover with cling film and place in the fridge to rest for 30 minutes.

3 To prepare the filling, place all the ingredients in a medium bowl and mix together with a fork. Place in the fridge to rest for 10 minutes

4 Flatten the prepared pasta dough with your fingers so that it can fit through the rollers of the pasta machine. Flour the pasta lightly on both sides and start to roll it

from the widest setting to the thinnest. Make sure you keep the pasta dusted with flour at all times. Lay the pasta sheets on a well-floured surface. Cut into discs using an 8cm cutter – you should get 28–30 discs.

5 Place about a teaspoonful of the filling in the middle of each disc, sharing it out equally. Brush the edges of the discs with beaten egg and fold over to make a half-moon shape. Press down to seal with your fingertips. Using a fork, press the edges again to secure the filling.

6 Heat the oil in a large saucepan until hot and smoking. Carefully drop in the sweet-filled pasta and fry for about 15 seconds until golden all over. (Be very careful and work in batches – no more than five mezzelune at a time.)

7 Once cooked, remove the mezzelune using a slotted spoon and place on some kitchen paper to soak up any excess oil.

8 To serve, place all the mezzelune on a large serving dish and dust with plenty of icing sugar. Serve warm with a little glass of Amaretto or Vin Santo.

PASTICCIO DOLCE
Sweet pasta cake with Amaretto liqueur

With this dessert, a lot of Italians will think that I've gone mad. In fact, when I had the boys, Marco, Leo and Franco, round one night I made a four course pasta feast and the dessert was this – they admitted that it tasted good but they laughed for about half an hour that I was actually making a dessert with pasta. I love it and am sure you will too. Please make sure you leave it to cool slightly so it sets properly and you can use chocolate chips instead of raisins if you prefer.

Serves 6
150g raisins
4 tablespoons Amaretto liqueur
3 Granny Smith apples
juice of ½ lemon
olive oil, for greasing
250g vermicelli or thin noodle pasta
4 eggs
130g caster sugar
80g almonds, chopped
zest of 1 orange
salt
4 tablespoons demerara sugar

1 Place the raisins in a small bowl and pour over the Amaretto. Leave to soak for 10 minutes.

2 Preheat the oven to 180°C/fan 160°C/gas mark 4.

3 Peel, core and coarsely grate the apples. Place in a bowl and squeeze over the lemon juice to prevent the apple turning brown.

4 Line a 20 x 20cm loaf tin with baking parchment and lightly brush with oil.

5 Cook the pasta in a large saucepan of boiling salted water until al dente. Drain and rinse under cold water. Set aside.

6 Meanwhile, put the eggs and sugar in a large bowl and lightly beat. Add in the almonds, orange zest and the raisins with the Amaretto. Fold in the pasta and the grated apples.

7 Pour the mixture into the loaf tin, cover with foil and bake for 40 minutes. Remove the foil, sprinkle with the demerara sugar and continue to bake for a further 10 minutes until lightly browned on top.

8 Remove from the oven and rest for 15 minutes.

9 Serve at room temperature with a touch of cream.

MEZZELUNE AL CIOCCOLATO
Half-moon shaped pasta filled with chocolate chips and hazelnuts

This is an amazing way of using pasta in a dessert dish. I know that it may sound a little difficult to prepare but trust me, once you've learned the technique, you will make this dish over and over again. Make sure you never serve this dish hot but always warm or at room temperature, as you will appreciate the flavours more.

Serves 6–8
3 eggs and 2 egg yolks
300g plain flour, plus extra for dusting
50g butter, softened
4 tablespoons Grand Marnier
1 litre vegetable oil, for deep frying
cocoa powder, for dusting

For the filling
40g caster sugar
250g ricotta cheese
zest of 1/2 orange, finely chopped
12 hazelnuts, finely chopped
50g good-quality dark chocolate, finely chopped

1 Beat 2 of the whole eggs in a bowl and set aside.

2 To make the dough, put the remaining egg and 2 egg yolks in a food processor. Add in the flour, the butter and the Grand Marnier. Process until the mixture just holds together.

3 Turn out the mixture onto a well-floured surface and knead for 2 minutes until you have a soft dough. Cover with cling film and place in the fridge to rest for 30 minutes.

4 To prepare the filling, place all the ingredients in a medium bowl and mix with a fork until combined. Place in the fridge to rest for 10 minutes.

5 Flatten the prepared dough with your fingers so that it can fit through the rollers of the pasta machine. Flour the pasta lightly on both sides and start to roll it from the widest setting to the thinnest. Make sure you keep the pasta dusted with flour at all times. Lay the sheets on a well-floured surface and cut into discs using an 8cm cutter. You should get about 28–30 discs in total.

6 Place about a teaspoonful of filling in the middle of each disc, sharing it out equally. Brush the edges of the discs with beaten egg and fold over to make a half-moon shape. Press down to seal with your fingertips. Using a fork, press the edges again to secure the filling.

7 Heat the oil in a saucepan until hot and smoking. Carefully drop in the sweet-filled pasta and fry for about 15 seconds until golden all over. (Take great care with the hot oil and do not fry more than five mezzelune at a time).

8 Once cooked, remove the mezzelune using a slotted spoon and place on some kitchen paper to soak up any excess oil.

9 Place the mezzelune on a large serving dish and dust with cocoa powder.

10 Serve warm – delicious with a little glass of Vin Santo.

LIKE MAMMA USED TO MAKE

GNOCCHETTI BURRO E SALVIA

Gnocchetti with courgettes in butter and sage sauce

My grandfather, nonno Giovanni, used to be the king of gnocchi. One of my earliest memories as a child is making potato dumplings with him in his kitchen and I really believe that was the start of my love affair with cooking. I know that this is a little bit fiddly but I promise that the effort is worth it and extremely satisfying. Please always use fresh sage and never the dried variety.

Serves 4 as a starter or 2 as a main
300g floury potatoes, unpeeled
1 small egg, lightly beaten
100g plain flour, plus extra for dusting
100g salted butter
2 medium courgettes, cut into 1cm cubes
1 tablespoon finely sliced fresh sage
30g freshly grated Parmesan cheese
salt and pepper to taste

1 Cook the whole potatoes in a large saucepan of boiling water for 25–30 minutes until tender. Drain well and cool slightly.

2 Peel the potatoes and press the flesh through a potato ricer into a large bowl. While the potatoes are still warm, add 2 pinches of salt, the egg and the flour. Lightly mix and then turn out onto a floured surface.

3 Knead lightly until you have a soft, slightly sticky dough. (Do not overwork it or the gnocchetti will be tough.)

4 Cut the dough into 2 and roll each piece into a long sausage shape, about 1.5cm in diameter. Cut into 2cm pieces.

5 Lay the gnocchetti on a lightly floured clean tea towel. Bring a large saucepan of salted water to the boil. Drop in the gnocchetti and cook for about 2 minutes – they are ready when they float to the surface. Remove from the water with a slotted spoon and drain.

6 Meanwhile melt the butter in a large frying pan over a medium heat. Once hot, add the courgettes and cook for 3 minutes before stirring in the sage. Season with salt and pepper and remove from the heat.

7 Place the gnocchetti in the frying pan and toss everything together.

8 Serve immediately, sprinkled with the Parmesan cheese.

LINGUINE CON GRANCHIO E LIMONE
Linguine with crab, fresh chilli and lemon zest

This is a great pasta dish that I learnt in the town of Amalfi approximately twenty years ago, when I had just started catering college. The secret is simple: all the ingredients must be fresh and the pasta has to be al dente. As you know by now, I hate cheese with most fish dishes so please refrain from adding it.

Serves 4
450g dressed crab, including the shell
5 tablespoons extra virgin olive oil
2 garlic cloves, peeled and finely chopped
1 medium-hot red chilli, deseeded and finely chopped
3 tablespoons freshly chopped flat leaf parsley
zest of 1 unwaxed lemon
3 tablespoons freshly squeezed lemon juice
500g linguine
salt to taste

1 Using a tablespoon, scoop out the crab meat from the shell and claws into a bowl and mix together the white and brown meat.

2 Heat the oil in a large frying pan over a low heat and fry the garlic and chilli together for 30 seconds.

3 Add in the crab with the parsley, lemon zest and juice. Cook for 1 minute until the crab is heated through. Season with salt and set aside.

4 Meanwhile cook the pasta in a large saucepan of boiling salted water until al dente. Drain and tip back into the same pan, off the heat. Spoon in the crab sauce and stir everything together for 30 seconds to allow the flavours to combine.

5 Serve immediately and please do not be tempted to serve it with grated cheese on top.

LINGUINE ALLA PUTTANESCA

Linguine with cherry tomatoes, anchovies and capers

OK guys this is how it goes ... 'Puttanesca' in Italian means a dish made by prostitutes. In the old days when the sailors were coming back to the port of Naples they used to be attracted by the local prostitutes who always used to prepare this dish to give them strength before a night of passion. Well, I really think there is nothing more to say – enjoy and I hope the old wives' tale works for you!

Serves 4

6 tablespoons olive oil
1 garlic clove, peeled and finely sliced
8 anchovy fillets in oil, drained and chopped
$1/2$ teaspoon dried chilli flakes
50g salted capers, rinsed under cold water
100g pitted Kalamata olives, halved
2 x 400g tins cherry tomatoes
500g linguine
salt to taste

1 Heat the oil in a large frying pan or wok over a medium heat and fry the garlic and anchovies for about 2 minutes, stirring occasionally with a wooden spoon. Add in the chilli, capers and olives and continue to cook for a further 3 minutes. Continue to stir.

2 Pour in the cherry tomatoes and stir well. Simmer gently for 8 minutes, uncovered, stirring every couple of minutes. Once ready, season with salt, remove from the heat and set aside.

3 Cook the pasta in a large saucepan of boiling salted water until al dente. Drain and tip back into the same pan. Pour in the sauce and stir everything together for 30 seconds to allow the flavours to combine.

4 Serve immediately without any kind of cheese sprinkled on top.

LASAGNE CON PESTO
Lasagne with pesto

I must have tasted at least thirty different lasagne recipes, so believe me when I say that this is the one to try. The fresh basil pesto melted into the béchamel sauce is just *fantastico*.

Serves 6–8
3 tablespoons olive oil
1 onion, peeled and finely chopped
1 large carrot, peeled and grated
1 celery stick, finely chopped
500g minced beef
1 glass of Italian dry red wine
700ml passata (sieved tomatoes)
1 tablespoon tomato purée
12 fresh lasagne sheets (each about 10 x 15cm)
50g cold salted butter, cut into 1cm cubes
salt and pepper to taste

For the béchamel sauce
100g salted butter
100g plain flour
1 litre cold full-fat milk
¼ teaspoon nutmeg, freshly grated
100g freshly grated Parmesan cheese

For the pesto
40g fresh basil leaves
1 garlic clove, peeled
30g pine nuts
120ml extra virgin olive oil
20g freshly grated Parmesan cheese
pinch of salt to taste

1 Preheat the oven to 180°C /fan 160°C/gas mark 4.

2 To prepare the pesto, place the basil, garlic and pine nuts in a food processor. Pour in the oil and blitz for about 10 seconds until smooth. Transfer the mixture into a bowl and fold in the cheese. Season with salt and set aside.

3 For the meat sauce, heat the olive oil in a large saucepan and cook the onions, carrot and celery for 5 minutes on a medium heat. Add in the minced beef and continue to cook for a further 5 minutes stirring continuously until coloured all over. Season with salt and pepper and cook for a further 5 minutes, stirring occasionally.

4 Pour in the wine, stir well and cook for about 3 minutes to allow the alcohol to evaporate. Add the passata and tomato purée, lower the heat and continue to cook for 1 hour, uncovered, until you get a beautiful rich sauce. Stir occasionally. After about 30 minutes, taste for seasoning.

5 Prepare the béchamel sauce as described on page 84. Once thickened, stir in half of the parmesan cheese, the nutmeg and the pesto. Season and set aside to slightly cool.

6 To assemble the lasagne, spread a quarter of the béchamel sauce over the bottom of a deep ovenproof dish measuring about 30 x 25cm and lay 4 lasagne sheets on top, trimming if necessary to fit the dish. Spread half the meat sauce over the lasagne then top with a third of the remaining béchamel sauce.

7 Lay 4 more sheets of lasagne on top and cover with the remaining meat sauce. Spread half the remaining béchamel sauce on top. Add a final layer of lasagne and gently spread the rest of the béchamel on top, completely covering all the lasagne sheets. Sprinkle with the remaining Parmesan and scatter over the cubed butter. Grind some black pepper over the whole lasagne.

8 Cook on the bottom shelf of the oven for 30 minutes then place in the middle of the oven and increase the temperature to 200°C/fan 180C/gas mark 6. Cook for a further 15 minutes until golden and crispy all over.

9 Once ready, leave it to rest for 5 minutes. It will be easier to cut and serve as the layers will hold together.

PENNE ALL' ARRABBIATA
Penne with red chillies, garlic and chopped tomatoes

This is the kind of pasta that I like to prepare when I'm on my own and I'm in need of something quick and tasty to eat. It is the ultimate Italian comfort food; food that satisfies every part of your body. Do not use fresh tomatoes for this sauce otherwise it will be too watery. If you prefer you can use dried chilli flakes instead of the fresh chillies.

Serves 4

6 tablespoons extra virgin olive oil
2 garlic cloves, peeled and chopped
2 medium-hot red chillies, deseeded and finely chopped
2 x 400g tins chopped tomatoes
3 tablespoons freshly chopped flat leaf parsley,
  plus extra to serve
500g penne rigate
salt to taste

1 Heat the oil in a large frying pan or a wok over a medium heat and add the garlic and chilli. Fry for about 1 minute, stirring with a wooden spoon.

2 Pour in the chopped tomatoes and parsley, stir well and simmer gently, uncovered, for 10 minutes, stirring every couple of minutes.

3 Once ready, season with salt, remove from the heat and set aside.

4 Meanwhile cook the pasta in a large saucepan of boiling salted water until al dente. Drain and tip back into the same pan.

5 Put the saucepan back over a low heat, pour in the Arrabbiata sauce and stir everything together for 1 minute to allow the flavours to combine.

6 Serve immediately sprinkled with chopped parsley and grated Parmesan if you wish.

PANZANELLA E PASTA
Northern Italian salad with roasted peppers and pasta

Panzanella is a traditional northern Italian salad which is mainly made with peppers, tomatoes, salad leaves and stale bread. My mother once made it into a pasta salad and although at the time I thought she was going crazy, I have to admit that it was, and still is, *fantastico!* You can substitute the penne pasta with fusilli or farfalle if you prefer.

Serves 4
3 red peppers
2 tablespoons olive oil, plus extra for drizzling
250g penne rigate
100g frisée lettuce, washed
100g radicchio, washed
1 small cucumber, cut into 1 cm cubes
1 large red onion, peeled and finely sliced
3 ripe tomatoes, roughly chopped
2 tablespoons capers in vinegar, drained
10 fresh basil leaves, roughly sliced
8 anchovy fillets in oil, drained and chopped

For the dressing
3 tablespoons red wine vinegar
5 tablespoons extra virgin olive oil
1 teaspoon sugar
salt and pepper to taste

1 Preheat the oven to 180°C/fan 160°C/gas mark 4. Place the whole peppers in a large roasting tin and drizzle over the olive oil. Roast for about 20 minutes until the skins are blackened all over. Remove from the oven, place in a large bowl and cover with cling film. Leave to rest for 10 minutes.

2 Once the roasted peppers have cooled sufficiently to handle, remove the skin, stalk and seeds and cut the flesh into strips. Set aside.

3 Cook the pasta in a large saucepan of boiling salted water until al dente. Drain the pasta through a colander and rinse under cold running water immediately, to stop the pasta cooking. Once cold, drizzle with olive oil and leave on the side to drain for 5 minutes. Give the pasta a good shake every minute or so.

4 Mix together the salad leaves, cucumber, onion, tomatoes, capers, basil and anchovies in a large bowl. Add in the pasta with the peppers.

5 Put all the ingredients for the dressing in a separate bowl and whisk together. Pour the dressing over the pasta salad and gently mix together.

6 Transfer the salad to a large serving dish and serve.

SPAGHETTI CON RICOTTA E PINOLI
Spaghetti with ricotta cheese and toasted pine nuts

This dish isn't what my mamma used to make but it is a recipe that my friend's mamma made beautifully. Every time I went to his house to play when I was younger I always begged her to make it for me. It is so full of flavour and to this day whenever I eat it, it takes me back to her house around a small kitchen table and reminds me of my childhood.

Serves 4

6 tablespoons pine nuts
250g ricotta cheese
100g sundried tomatoes in oil, drained and cut into thin strips
3 tablespoons finely chopped fresh chives
1/4 teaspoon freshly grated nutmeg
10 fresh basil leaves, chopped, plus extra to serve
4 tablespoons extra virgin olive oil
2 tablespoons hot water
500g spaghetti
salt and pepper to taste

1 Heat a dry frying pan and toast the pine nuts until golden brown all over. Watch carefully as they burn easily. Set aside.

2 Place the ricotta cheese in a large bowl with the sundried tomatoes, chives, nutmeg, pine nuts and basil. Pour over the oil and the hot water and season with salt and pepper. Mix everything together and allow to rest at room temperature.

3 Meanwhile cook the pasta in a large saucepan of boiling salted water until al dente. Drain and tip into the large bowl with the ricotta mixture. Gently fold everything together for 30 seconds to combine the ricotta mixture with the pasta.

4 Serve immediately.

PASTA E FASUL
Spicy pasta with borlotti and cannellini beans

Every time I cook this dish, there is only one person in my mind and that's my mother, Alba. I have to admit that she doesn't have a large recipe collection but this is by far her signature dish. Whenever I go back to Italy, she will always make me my spicy pasta with beans to remind me of home. If you fancy, you can substitute the pasta shells with any small tube shape pasta and if you are vegetarian you can certainly do without the pancetta.

Serves 4

5 tablespoons olive oil
200g diced pancetta
2 tablespoons freshly chopped rosemary leaves
1/2 teaspoon dried chilli flakes
1 x 400g tin borlotti beans
2 x 400g tins cannellini beans
2 good-quality vegetable stock cubes
1 litre boiling water
300g medium pasta shells (look for conchiglie)
salt to taste

1 Heat the oil in a large saucepan over a medium heat and cook the pancetta for 5 minutes. Stir occasionally with a wooden spoon.

2 Add in the rosemary and the chilli and continue to cook for a further 2 minutes.

3 Pour in the beans with the juices from the tins, stir everything together and cook for 5 minutes.

4 Add in the stock cubes with the boiling water. Stir, lower the heat and allow to simmer for 15 minutes with the lid half on. Stir every 5 minutes.

5 Add the pasta to the saucepan and cook the pasta in the bean sauce over a low heat. Season to taste. If the sauce looks too thick stir in a glass of hot water from the kettle.

6 Once the pasta is al dente, turn off the heat and allow to rest for 2 minutes before serving.

7 Divide the pasta between four serving bowls and enjoy with a glass of good red wine.

SPAGHETTI AGLIO, OLIO E PEPERONCINO
Spaghetti with garlic, olive oil and chilli

If you fancy making yourself a really special meal, this is the recipe for you – easy, spicy and full of flavours.

Serves 4
6 tablespoons extra virgin olive oil
3 garlic cloves, peeled and finely sliced
1 medium-hot red chilli, deseeded and finely chopped
6 tablespoons freshly chopped flat leaf parsley
500g spaghetti
salt to taste

1 Heat the oil in a large frying pan over a low heat and fry the garlic for about 1 minute until golden.

2 Add in the chilli and the parsley with 6 tablespoons of the salted water from the saucepan in which you will cook the pasta. Mix and set aside.

3 Cook the pasta in a large saucepan with plenty of boiling salted water until al dente. Drain and tip back into the pan.

4 Pour in the chilli and garlic oil and stir over a medium heat for 30 seconds to allow the flavours to combine.

5 Serve immediately without any kind of cheese sprinkled on top.

LINGUINE CON IMPEPATA DI COZZE
Linguine with mussels, garlic and white wine

There is a little place in the south of Italy called Castellammare where you can find the best and juiciest mussels in the world. The way they prepare them is so simple that I had to share this recipe with you. Make sure you use a good-quality dry white wine and, if you like, you can add a little chilli. Whatever you do though, do not put any kind of grated cheese on top.

Serves 4
800g mussels
150ml dry white wine
6 tablespoons extra virgin olive oil
2 garlic cloves, peeled and sliced
10 cherry tomatoes, halved
4 tablespoons freshly chopped flat leaf parsley
500g linguine
salt and pepper to taste

1 Wash the mussels under cold water, discard any broken ones and those that do not close when tapped firmly.

2 Place the mussels in a large saucepan, pour over the wine and cook, covered, over a medium heat for 5 minutes, until they have opened. Discard any that remain closed. Tip into a colander placed over a bowl to catch the cooking liquor and set aside. Reserve the cooking liquor for later.

3 Heat the oil in the same saucepan that you cooked the mussels and gently fry the garlic until it begins to sizzle. Add in the tomatoes and parsley and pour in the reserved cooking liquor from the mussels. Cook over a medium heat for 2 minutes. Season with salt and plenty of black pepper.

4 Meanwhile cook the pasta in a large saucepan of boiling salted water until al dente. Drain and tip into the saucepan with the sauce and the mussels.

5 Gently mix everything together over a low heat for 30 seconds to allow the sauce to coat the pasta evenly.

6 Serve immediately.

MINESTRONE ALLA MILANESE
Chunky vegetable and pasta soup

If you like traditional Italian soup, this is the one to have. There are three good things that come from Milan:- number one: Veal alla Milanese, number two: Silvio Berlusconi, the Italian prime minister, and finally number three: Minestrone alla Milanese. A chunky vegetable soup that never fails to impress in flavour, look and ease of preparation. If you prefer, you can do without the pasta but instead serve with some warm crusty bread.

Serves 6

2 carrots, peeled and cut into 1 cm cubes
3 celery sticks, cut into 1 cm cubes
100g green cabbage, roughly sliced
1 baking potato, peeled and cut into 1 cm cubes
2 onions, peeled and roughly chopped
6 tablespoons extra virgin olive oil
2 litres vegetable stock, made with 3 good-quality
   vegetable stock cubes
2 courgettes, cut into 1 cm cubes
300g tiny shell pasta (look for conchigliette)
15 fresh basil leaves
2 garlic cloves, peeled
80g freshly grated Parmesan cheese
salt and pepper to taste

1 Put the prepared carrots, celery, cabbage, potato and onions in a large saucepan. Pour in the oil and fry over a medium heat for 3 minutes, stirring occasionally with a wooden spoon.

2 Stir in the stock and, once it starts to boil, add the courgettes. Lower the heat and simmer for 15 minutes. Season to taste with salt and pepper and stir occasionally.

3 Add the pasta and continue to cook, uncovered, for about 6 minutes until the pasta is al dente. Stir every 2 minutes. Once the pasta is cooked, remove from the heat.

4 Put the basil in a food processor with the garlic and measure in 8 tablespoons of the hot liquid from the vegetables. Blitz to give a smooth runny paste.

5 Pour the basil paste into the saucepan with the pasta and vegetables. Stir until everything is well combined and check the seasoning.

6 Divide the minestrone between six serving bowls, sprinkle over the Parmesan and serve immediately.

FUSILLI AI QUATTRO FORMAGGI
Fusilli with four cheeses and chives

If you love cheese, this is the dish for you. I have chosen very strong flavoured cheeses (all my favourites) and hoped that it would work without them overpowering each other, which it does. It will not disappoint you. It is a heavy dish, but so tasty that you will find that you still go for seconds. My grandmother used to make it for me and I love the fact that I am now making it for my family and friends. Perfect accompanied with a cold beer.

Serves 4

250ml full-fat milk
800g Gorgonzola cheese, cubed
80g Cheddar cheese, grated
4 tablespoons finely chopped fresh chives
1 teaspoon cayenne pepper
500g fusilli
1 mozzarella ball, drained and cubed
60g freshly grated Parmesan cheese
salt to taste

1 Pour the milk into a medium saucepan and add the Gorgonzola and Cheddar. Set over a medium heat and gently melt the cheeses in the milk, stirring with a wooden spoon.

2 Once the cheeses have melted, add in the chives and the cayenne pepper and season with a little salt. Set aside.

3 Cook the pasta in a large saucepan of boiling salted water until al dente. Drain and tip back into the pan over a low heat.

4 Pour in the cheese sauce together with the mozzarella and Parmesan. Stir everything together for 30 seconds to allow the flavours to combine and the sauce to thicken.

5 Serve hot.

SPAGHETTI AL POMODORO
Spaghetti with basil and tomato sauce

A pasta dish loved by all, which happens to be my wife's favourite. I try to come up with amazing sauces and although she likes them all, Jessie will always have this one by choice. My family seem to smother the pasta with Parmesan cheese, the more the better for them, but if the tomatoes are good quality and the basil is fresh, you really need nothing else and I'm yet to meet a child that doesn't like it.

Serves 4
6 tablespoons extra virgin olive oil
1 onion, peeled and finely chopped
2 x 400g tins chopped tomatoes
10 fresh basil leaves
500g spaghetti
salt and pepper to taste

1 Heat the oil in a medium saucepan over a low heat and fry the onion for about 3 minutes until golden, stirring with a wooden spoon.

2 Pour in the tomatoes and basil, season with salt and pepper and cook, uncovered, over a medium heat for 15 minutes, stirring every 5 minutes.

3 Cook the pasta in a large saucepan of boiling salted water until al dente. Drain and tip back into the same pan.

4 Pour in the tomato and basil sauce and stir everything together for 30 seconds to allow the flavours to combine.

5 Serve immediately.

CONCHIGLIE RIGATE PICCANTI
Shell pasta with spicy pork and tomato sauce

I love this shape of pasta and this sauce is perfect for it. The delicate taste of the pork with the strong flavours of the chilli, olives and sun-dried tomatoes is a match made in heaven. I know that most people add cheese to pasta sauces but please don't to this one. It really doesn't need it and will actually ruin the natural flavours of the ingredients. If you fancy, substitute the conchiglie rigate with rigatoni.

Serves 4
5 tablespoons olive oil
1 onion, peeled and finely chopped
80g pitted Kalamata olives, halved
1 hot red chilli, deseeded and finely chopped
80g sun-dried tomatoes in oil, drained and
    finely chopped
300g minced pork
300g passata (sieved tomatoes)
400g medium shell pasta (look for conchiglie rigate)
salt to taste

1 Heat the oil in a medium saucepan or wok over a medium heat and fry the onion and olives for 2 minutes, stirring occasionally with a wooden spoon.

2 Add the chilli, sun-dried tomatoes and the minced pork and continue to fry for a further 6 minutes, stirring occasionally.

3 Stir in the passata then gently simmer, uncovered, for 15 minutes, stirring every couple of minutes. Season with salt and set aside, away from the heat.

4 Meanwhile cook the pasta in a large saucepan of boiling salted water until al dente. Drain and tip back into the same pan.

5 Pour in the sauce and stir everything together over a low heat for 30 seconds to allow the flavours to combine and the sauce to coat the pasta evenly.

6 Serve immediately without any kind of cheese on top.

SPAGHETTI CON VONGOLE
Spaghetti with clams, garlic and chilli

If you ask me what is a traditional dish from Torre del Greco, the town where I was born, it has to be pasta with clams. Every southern Italian family has their own variation of the recipe but this is the one I was brought up with and I wouldn't change it for anything else in the world. You can substitute the spaghetti with linguine but please never never never use tinned clams – they are disgusting. Perfect with a glass of cold Prosecco.

Serves 4
700g clams
6 tablespoons extra virgin olive oil
2 garlic cloves, peeled and sliced
1/2 teaspoon dried chilli flakes
4 tablespoons freshly chopped flat leaf parsley
500g spaghetti
salt to taste

1 Wash the clams under cold running water, discarding any broken ones and any that do not close when tapped firmly.

2 Place the clams in a large lidded saucepan and cook over a medium heat, covered, for 3 minutes until they have opened. Discard any that remain closed. Tip into a colander placed over a bowl and set aside. Reserve the liquor from the clams.

3 Pour the oil into the same saucepan that you used to cook the clams and gently fry the garlic until it begins to sizzle. Add the chilli and the parsley and pour in the reserved liquor. Cook over a medium heat for 2 minutes. Season with salt.

4 Meanwhile cook the pasta in a large saucepan of boiling salted water until al dente. Drain and tip into the pan with the sauce and the clams.

5 Gently mix all the ingredients together on a low heat for 30 seconds allowing the sauce to coat the pasta evenly.

6 Serve immediately.

LINGUINE ALLA AMATRICIANA

Linguine with cherry tomatoes, pancetta and white wine

With no doubt, I have to dedicate this recipe to my friend and manager, Jeremy Hicks. We have known each other for seven years now and without fail he has to have this pasta dish at least once a week. I actually agree with him, it's one of my favourites too, because I just love the combination of the onion, pancetta and chilli. If you prefer you can substitute linguine with spaghetti or tagliatelle.

Serves 4

4 tablespoons olive oil
1 large red onion, peeled and finely sliced
250g diced pancetta
100ml dry white wine
2 x 400g tins cherry tomatoes
1/2 teaspoon dried chilli flakes
500g linguine
3 tablespoons freshly chopped flat leaf parsley
100g freshly grated Pecorino Romano cheese
salt to taste

1 Heat the oil in a large frying pan or wok over a medium heat and fry the onion for about 5 minutes, stirring occasionally with a wooden spoon. Add the pancetta and continue to cook for a further 3 minutes. Pour in the wine and cook for a further 2 minutes to allow the alcohol to evaporate.

2 Add the cherry tomatoes and chilli, stir well and gently simmer for 8 minutes, uncovered, stirring every couple of minutes. Once the sauce is ready, season with salt, remove from the heat and set aside.

3 Cook the pasta in a large saucepan of boiling salted water until al dente. Drain and tip back into the same pan. Pour in the sauce and add the parsley; stir everything together for 30 seconds to allow the flavours to combine.

4 Serve immediately, sprinkled with the Pecorino Romano cheese.

BUCATINI ALLA CARBONARA
Bucatini with eggs, pancetta and Pecorino Romano

This has to be one of my favourite recipes ever, especially with this shape of pasta. Bucatini is like a thick spaghetti with a hole in the middle that runs from one end to the other. This allows the sauce to really coat the pasta inside and out beautifully. If you are a fan of a simple spaghetti dish, I recommend you try this traditional Roman recipe. You can substitute the pancetta with streaky bacon but please, never add cream to this sauce.

Serves 4

250g piece of smoked pancetta
2 tablespoons extra virgin olive oil
15g salted butter
4 eggs
4 tablespoons freshly grated Pecorino Romano
4 tablespoons finely chopped fresh flat leaf parsley
500g bucatini
salt and pepper to taste

1 Cut the pancetta into short little strips about 0.5cm wide.

2 Heat the oil and butter in a large frying pan or wok over a medium heat and fry the pancetta for about 5 minutes until golden and crispy. Stir occasionally and, once ready, remove from the heat and set aside.

3 Whisk the eggs in a bowl with half of the cheese. Add in the parsley and plenty of black pepper.

4 Cook the pasta in a large saucepan of boiling salted water until al dente. Drain and tip back into the saucepan.

5 Add in the pancetta and pour over the egg mixture. Mix everything together for 30 seconds with a wooden spoon. (The heat from the pasta will be sufficient to cook the egg to a creamy texture.)

6 Season with salt and pepper and serve immediately with the remaining cheese sprinkled on top.

PASTA
ON THE GO

FUSILLI CON GAMBERETTI
Fusilli with prawns and basil pesto

I love prawns and usually make a sauce with prawns, garlic and rocket leaves, but one night I wanted to use up a half-opened jar of pesto and some tomatoes and came up with this amazing meal. The freshness of the pesto slightly mellowed by the tomatoes, together with the sweet prawns, makes this the ultimate pasta salad. Of course you can also serve this hot but it works beautifully for a takeaway lunch.

Serves 4
400g fusilli
4 tablespoons olive oil
4 tablespoons good-quality pesto Genovese
  (see page 62)
250g prawns, cooked and peeled
10 cherry tomatoes, halved
salt and pepper to taste

1 Measure 4 litres of water into a large saucepan and bring to the boil with 3 tablespoons of salt. Add the pasta and cook until al dente.

2 Drain the pasta through a colander and rinse under cold running water immediately, to stop the pasta cooking. Once cold, drizzle over the oil and leave on the side to drain for 5 minutes. Give the pasta a good shake every minute or so.

3 Meanwhile place the rest of the ingredients in a large bowl.

4 Add the pasta to the bowl and gently mix everything together to allow the flavours to combine.

5 Leave to rest at room temperature for 5 minutes. Stir occasionally.

6 Once ready, serve immediately or keep in a sealed container in the fridge for the following day. Do not keep longer than 48 hours and always eat it at room temperature.

TOFE CON FAGIOLINI E POMODORINI
Shell pasta with green beans and cherry tomatoes

What a great vegetarian dish – full of flavours, colours and of course, most importantly, very simple to prepare. I sometimes make this pasta when I'm not sure if my guests are vegetarian or not. Even someone who loves meat will like this. You can substitute the cherry tomatoes with sun-dried tomatoes and make sure that you don't use buffalo mozzarella because it will break down and become too runny.

Serves 4

500g medium pasta shells (look for tofe, which are about the right size)
250g green beans, trimmed and cut into quarters
100g fresh peas (if not in season you can use frozen ones)
8 tablespoons extra virgin olive oil, plus extra for drizzling
250g cherry tomatoes, halved
2 shallots, peeled and sliced into rings
2 mozzarella balls, drained and cut into small cubes
2 tablespoons finely chopped fresh marjoram leaves
50g freshly grated Pecorino cheese
salt and pepper to taste

1 Measure 4 litres of water into a large saucepan and bring to the boil with 2 tablespoons of salt.

2 Cook the pasta with the green beans and peas in the salted boiling water until al dente.

3 Drain the pasta, beans and peas through a colander and rinse under cold running water immediately, to stop the pasta cooking. Once cold, leave on the side to drain for 5 minutes. Drizzle with a little olive oil and give the pasta a good shake every minute or so.

4 Meanwhile place the tomatoes, shallots, mozzarella and marjoram in a large bowl. Pour over the extra virgin olive oil, season with salt and pepper and mix together.

5 Add the pasta, beans and peas to the bowl, sprinkle over the Pecorino cheese and gently mix everything together to allow the flavours to combine.

6 Cover with cling film and leave to rest at room temperature for 15 minutes. Stir every 5 minutes.

7 Serve immediately or keep in a sealed container in the fridge for the day after. Do not keep longer than 48 hours and always eat it at room temperature.

FRITTATA DI SPAGHETTI
Spaghetti frittata with Parmesan and rocket

When I was fourteen and I got my first scooter, I used to go to the beach with my friends during the summer and my mother always used to do the same packed lunch for me – Frittata di Spaghetti. I can still remember the flavours and no matter how much she used to pack for me there was never any left over. This dish is even better the day after it's made once the flavours have developed. You can substitute spaghetti for linguine if you fancy.

Serves 4
300g spaghetti
4 large eggs
150g rocket, roughly chopped
100g sun-dried tomatoes in oil, drained and chopped
80g freshly grated Parmesan cheese
6 tablespoons olive oil
salt and pepper to taste

1 Cook the pasta in a large saucepan of boiling salted water until al dente. Drain into a colander and rinse under cold running water immediately, to stop the pasta cooking. Once cold, leave on the side to drain for 5 minutes. Give the pasta a good shake every minute or so.

2 Preheat the oven to 180°C/fan 160°C/gas mark 4.

3 Break the eggs into a large bowl and add in the rocket, sun-dried tomatoes and the grated Parmesan. Season with salt and pepper and mix together.

4 Add the pasta to the egg mixture, mix and leave to rest for 5 minutes.

5 Meanwhile pour the oil in a 22cm baking dish with sides about 5cm deep. Ensure the dish is well coated with oil. Pour in the pasta mixture and spread it out evenly.

6 Cook in the middle of the preheated oven for 20 minutes until crispy and set. Remove from the oven and allow to rest for 2 minutes before cutting into portions.

7 Serve warm or at room temperature.

CONCHIGLIE CON ZUCCHINE E PANCETTA
Shell pasta with courgettes, garlic and pancetta

A pasta dish that screams summer every time I make it. I remember whenever I was in Italy and courgettes were in season, my grandfather used to make this dish at least once a week and if we didn't fancy the sauce with the pasta, we used to put it on top of toasted bread and have it as a starter. I still use the courgette sauce to go on my jacket potato with a little sprinkle of Cheddar cheese on top.

Serves 4

150ml olive oil
3 large courgettes, trimmed and cut into sticks about
  1cm wide and 3cm long
150g cubed pancetta
2 garlic cloves, peeled and halved
2 x 400g tins chopped tomatoes
4 tablespoons freshly chopped flat leaf parsley
500g medium shell pasta (look for conchiglie)
salt and pepper to taste

1 Heat the oil in a large frying pan over a medium heat, add in the courgettes and fry for 5 minutes until golden and crispy on both sides.

2 Use a slotted spoon to remove the courgettes from the pan and drain on kitchen paper. Sprinkle with a little salt.

3 Discard two-thirds of the oil from the frying pan, return to a medium heat and fry the pancetta with the garlic in the remaining oil for 3 minutes. Stir in the tomatoes and the parsley and simmer for 10 minutes, stirring occasionally with a wooden spoon.

4 Add the courgettes to the pan, stir and continue to cook for a further 5 minutes. Season with salt and pepper and set aside.

5 Meanwhile cook the pasta in a large saucepan of boiling salted water until al dente. Drain and tip back into the same pan over a low heat.

6 Pour in the courgette sauce and stir everything together for 30 seconds to allow the sauce to coat the pasta evenly.

7 Serve immediately or cool to room temperature, transfer to a sealed container and store in the fridge for the day after. Do not keep longer than 48 hours and always eat it at room temperature.

FARFALLE CON NOCI E GORGONZOLA
Pasta salad with walnuts and Gorgonzola cheese

Gorgonzola and walnuts have always been a great combination. I find that they work perfectly with pasta and rocket. Of course you can eat this dish hot, but if you are making it for the following day make sure you eat it at room temperature and mix well before serving. If you prefer, substitute the Gorgonzola with any hard blue cheese of your choice.

Serves 4
500g farfalle
8 tablespoons extra virgin olive oil, plus extra for drizzling
250g cold Gorgonzola cheese, cut into 1cm cubes
100g walnut halves
200g rocket
2 tablespoons balsamic vinegar
salt and pepper to taste

1 Pour 4 litres of water into a large saucepan and bring to the boil with 2 tablespoons salt.

2 Cook the pasta in the large saucepan of boiling salted water until al dente. Drain the pasta through a colander and rinse under cold running water immediately, to stop the pasta cooking. Once cold, drizzle with oil and leave on the side to drain for 5 minutes. Give the pasta a good shake every minute or so.

3 Meanwhile place the Gorgonzola, walnuts and rocket in a large bowl. Pour over 8 tablespoons of extra virgin olive oil and the balsamic vinegar. Season with salt and pepper and mix thoroughly.

4 Add the pasta to the bowl and gently toss everything together to allow the flavours to combine.

5 Cover with cling film and leave to rest at room temperature for 5 minutes. Stir every 2 minutes.

6 Serve immediately or keep in a sealed container in the fridge for the following day. Do not keep longer than 48 hours and always eat it at room temperature.

PASTIERA DI MACCHERONI

Pasta bake with pancetta, rosemary and minced pork

In my family we have to do this pasta dish at least once a week simply because my boys, Luciano and Rocco, absolutely love it. Believe me, although the recipe is for six people, there is never any left over for my chickens. This is not one just for the kids though – it's the ultimate boys' dinner, which should be accompanied by a good cold beer.

Serves 6

6 tablespoons extra virgin olive oil
1 red onion, peeled and finely chopped
1 carrot, peeled and finely chopped
250g cubed pancetta
500g minced pork
2 tablespoons freshly chopped rosemary
1 x 400g tin cherry tomatoes
300g penne rigate
4 large eggs
50g freshly grated Parmesan cheese
salt and pepper to taste

1 Heat 4 tablespoons of the olive oil in a large saucepan and fry the onion and carrot for 5 minutes until soft. Stir occasionally with a wooden spoon.

2 Add the pancetta with the minced pork and rosemary and continue to cook for a further 5 minutes, stirring continuously until coloured all over.

3 Pour in the tomatoes, season with salt and pepper and continue to cook over a medium heat for 15 minutes. Stir occasionally. Once ready set aside to allow the sauce to cool to room temperature.

4 Meanwhile cook the pasta in a large saucepan of boiling salted water until al dente. Drain and add to the meat sauce. Stir well and leave to cool.

5 Preheat the oven to 180°C/fan 160°C/gas mark 4.

6 Break the eggs into the saucepan of cooled pasta and add in the grated Parmesan. Mix together.

7 Brush the remaining oil over the sides and base of a 22cm roundish nonstick baking dish with sides about 5cm deep. Pour in the pasta mixture and spread out evenly.

8 Cook in the centre of the preheated oven for 20 minutes until crispy and set.

9 Once cooked, leave it to rest for 5 minutes. It will be easier to cut and serve as the layers will hold together. Serve hot or cold.

FUSILLI CON CREMA DI OLIVE
Fusilli with black olive tapenade

A very seasonal southern Italian recipe, which you will find during September and October when the olive harvest takes place. It is great for a picnic and to take to the office, making everybody jealous! If you fancy, you can substitute the parsley with fresh mint.

Serves 4
500g fusilli
250g pitted Kalamata olives, drained
2 garlic cloves, peeled
30g salted capers, rinsed and drained
3 tablespoons freshly chopped flat leaf parsley
5 tablespoons extra virgin olive oil
2 tablespoons freshly squeezed lemon juice

1 Cook the pasta in a large saucepan of boiling salted water until al dente. Drain through a colander and rinse under cold running water immediately, to stop the pasta cooking. Once cold leave on the side to drain for 5 minutes. Give the pasta a good shake every minute or so.

2 Meanwhile place the olives, garlic, capers and parsley in a food processor. Pour in the oil and the lemon juice and start to blitz to create a smooth paste. If the tapenade is too dry, add a little cold water to loosen it up. Place in a large bowl.

3 Add the pasta to the bowl with the tapenade and gently toss everything together to allow the flavours to combine. Cover with cling film and leave to rest at room temperature for 15 minutes. Stir every 5 minutes.

4 Serve immediately or transfer to a sealed container and store in the fridge for the day after. Do not keep longer than 48 hours and always eat it at room temperature.

PENNE CON ZUCCHINE E SALMONE

Penne with courgettes, smoked salmon and lemon zest

This dish is excellent if you are not keen on fishy flavours. I know that it works because my wife Jessie doesn't really like any kind of fish and yet this is one of her favourite recipes.

Serves 2

2 courgettes, trimmed
5 tablespoons olive oil
1/2 teaspoon dried chilli flakes
2 tablespoons pine nuts
150g smoked salmon, roughly chopped
250g penne rigate
zest of 1/2 unwaxed lemon
2 tablespoons finely chopped fresh chives
salt to taste

1 Coarsely grate the courgettes and place in the middle of a clean tea towel. Squeeze over a sink, allowing all the water from the courgettes to run out.

2 Heat the oil in a large frying pan over a medium heat and fry the courgettes for 3 minutes, stirring continuously to ensure they cook evenly. Add the chilli flakes, pine nuts and smoked salmon and continue to cook for a further 5 minutes. Season with salt and set aside.

3 Meanwhile cook the pasta in a large saucepan of boiling salted water until al dente. Drain and tip back into the same pan.

4 Add the courgette mixture to the pasta with the lemon zest and chives and toss everything together over a medium heat for 30 seconds.

5 Serve immediately or cool to room temperature, transfer to a sealed container and store in the fridge for the day after. Do not keep longer than 48 hours and always eat it at room temperature.

RIGATONI CON MELANZANE E POMODORINI
Rigatoni with aubergines, garlic and cherry tomatoes

I know that many of you are scared of aubergines but please trust me when I say that this is the easiest and yet the most beautiful recipe to make. The flavour of the fried aubergines with the cherry tomatoes is absolutely divine. This is a fantastic dish to use for dinner parties. It is important to only use fresh basil leaves, as dried ones will ruin the dish.

Serves 4

2 medium aubergines, trimmed
150ml olive oil
3 garlic cloves, peeled and halved
2 x 400g tins cherry tomatoes
10 fresh basil leaves
500g rigatoni
salt and pepper to taste

1 Place the aubergines on a chopping board and cut in half lengthways, then into quarters and then sticks about 1cm wide, discarding the centre part containing the seeds.

2 Heat the oil in a large frying pan, add the aubergines and fry for about 5 minutes until golden brown and crispy.

3 Use a slotted spoon to remove the aubergines from the pan and drain on kitchen paper. Sprinkle with a little salt.

4 Discard two-thirds of the oil from the pan and fry the garlic in the remaining oil for 30 seconds. Add the cherry tomatoes with the basil, stir everything together and simmer over a medium heat for 10 minutes, stirring occasionally.

5 Return the aubergines to the pan, stir and continue to cook for a further 5 minutes. Season with salt and pepper and set aside.

6 Cook the pasta in a large saucepan of boiling salted water until al dente. Drain and tip back into the same pan.

7 Return the pan to a low heat, pour in the sauce and stir everything together for 30 seconds to allow the flavours to combine.

8 Serve immediately or cool to room temperature, transfer to a sealed container and store in the fridge for the following day. Do not keep longer than 48 hours and always eat it at room temperature.

FARFALLINE TONNO E FAGIOLI
Three bean and tuna pasta salad

I used to make this recipe without the pasta. Tuna and bean salad is amazing all year round. I was having a few friends round for lunch once and wanted to make lots of different dishes. I tried adding farfalline to the tuna salad to make it a more substantial meal and it was a massive hit. It's such a tasty dish and not only extremely healthy but hugely filling too!

Serves 6
300g farfalline
1 x 400g tin chick peas, drained
1 x 400g tin red kidney beans, drained
1 x 400g tin butter beans, drained
2 x 200g tins tuna in oil, drained
1 red onion, peeled and finely sliced
1 unwaxed lemon
6 tablespoons extra virgin olive oil
2 tablespoons freshly chopped mint leaves
salt and pepper to taste

1 Pour 4 litres of water into a large saucepan and bring to the boil with 2 tablespoons salt. Cook the pasta in the boiling salted water until al dente. Drain the pasta through a colander and rinse under cold running water immediately, to stop the pasta cooking. Once cold leave on the side to drain for 5 minutes. Give the pasta a good shake every minute or so.

2 Place all the beans in a large bowl with the tuna and the sliced onion. Squeeze over the juice of half the lemon and pour in the oil. Add in the mint and season with salt and pepper. Mix everything together and leave to rest for 5 minutes at room temperature.

3 Add the pasta to the bowl with the beans and gently toss everything together to allow the flavours to combine. Cover with cling film and leave to rest at room temperature for 15 minutes. Stir every 5 minutes.

4 Serve immediately or transfer to a sealed container and store in the fridge for the day after. Do not keep longer than 48 hours and always eat it at room temperature.

PENNE ALLA CRUDAIOLA

Penne with feta cheese, cherry tomatoes and mint

If you are in a rush and need to prepare something quickly, putting this plate of pasta together couldn't be simpler. I have taken the concept of a traditional Italian sauce but just by changing the type of cheese and adding mint, this dish becomes extremely fresh, light and yet still filling. The feta and mint are a fantastic Mediterranean combination and this recipe will not disappoint you.

Serves 4

5 tablespoons extra virgin olive oil
1 garlic clove, peeled and finely sliced
300g cherry tomatoes, halved
400g penne rigate
10 fresh mint leaves, finely sliced
150g feta cheese, drained and cubed
salt and pepper to taste

1 Heat the oil in a frying pan and gently fry the garlic and cherry tomatoes for 1 minute, stirring with a wooden spoon. Season with salt and pepper and set aside, away from the heat.

2 Meanwhile cook the pasta in a large saucepan of boiling salted water until al dente. Drain and tip back into the same pan.

3 Pour in the garlic and tomatoes and add the mint and feta cheese. Toss everything together, away from the heat, for 30 seconds to allow the flavours to combine.

4 Serve immediately or cool to room temperature, transfer to a sealed container and store in the fridge for the following day. Do not keep longer than 48 hours and always eat it at room temperature.

CONCHIGLIE ALLA CAPRESE

Shell pasta with tomato, mozzarella and fresh basil

Back to simple yet perfect combinations. The traditional, yet never tired, mozzarella, basil and tomato. It just shouts fresh, tasty and Italian. Try and buy the freshest cherry tomatoes you possibly can and buffalo mozzarella is best for this dish. If you prefer, you can substitute the shell pasta with fusilli or farfalle.

Serves 4

20 cherry tomatoes, halved
15 fresh basil leaves
3 mozzarella balls, drained and cut into 1cm cubes
8 tablespoons extra virgin olive oil
400g medium shell pasta (look for conchiglie)
salt and pepper to taste

1 Place the tomatoes, basil and mozzarella in a large bowl. Drizzle over the oil and season with salt and pepper. Mix and set aside while you cook the pasta.

2 Measure 4 litres of water into a large saucepan and bring to the boil with 3 tablespoons of salt. Cook the pasta in the boiling salted water until al dente. Drain the pasta through a colander and rinse under cold running water immediately, to stop the pasta cooking. Once cold leave on the side to drain for 5 minutes. Give the pasta a good shake every minute or so.

3 Add the pasta to the bowl with the tomato mixture and gently mix everything together to allow the flavours to combine.

4 Leave to rest at room temperature for 10 minutes. Stir every couple of minutes.

5 Serve immediately or cool to room temperature, transfer to a sealed container and store in the fridge for the day after. Do not keep longer than 48 hours and always eat it at room temperature.

PENNE ALLA CALABRESE
Penne with cherry tomatoes, garlic, olives and capers

When I was a boy, I used to go to camping with my family in Calabria and this plate of pasta is what I remember most from those fun days. The secret is very simple: fresh and good-quality ingredients. Do not try and use dried basil as it spoils the dish. If you prefer, you can substitute the pitted black olives with green ones.

Serves 4

4 tablespoons extra virgin olive oil
250g cherry tomatoes, quartered
2 tablespoons salted capers, rinsed under cold water
2 garlic cloves, peeled and finely chopped
10 pitted Kalamata olives, chopped
3 tablespoons pine nuts
100g sun-dried tomatoes in oil, drained and cut
  into strips
500g penne
10 fresh basil leaves
salt and pepper to taste

1 Heat the oil in a large frying pan over a medium heat and gently fry the cherry tomatoes for 1 minute, stirring with a wooden spoon.

2 Add in the capers, garlic, olives, pine nuts and sun-dried tomatoes. Continue to fry for a further 3 minutes, stirring continuously. Season with salt and pepper and set aside.

3 Meanwhile cook the pasta in a large saucepan of boiling salted water until al dente. Drain and tip back into the same pan.

4 Pour in the sauce with the basil and stir everything together for 30 seconds to allow the flavours to combine.

5 Serve immediately or cool to room temperature, transfer to a sealed container and store in the fridge for the following day. Do not keep longer than 48 hours and always eat it at room temperature.

FUSILLI CON ZUCCHINE ALLA SCAPECE
Pasta salad with courgettes and balsamic vinegar

If I had to choose one thing that I have in common with my father, it would have to be our love of this dish. We both adore courgettes and are both big fans of balsamic vinegar. A little tip for you – you can also use the courgette sauce as a topping for bruschetta.

Serves 4
400g fusilli
5 tablespoons extra virgin olive oil, plus extra for drizzling
2 large courgettes
3 tablespoons balsamic vinegar
2 garlic cloves, peeled and thinly sliced
15 fresh mint leaves
100g feta cheese, cut into 1cm cubes
salt and pepper to taste

1 Cook the pasta in a large saucepan of boiling salted water until al dente. Drain the pasta through a colander and rinse under cold running water immediately, to stop the pasta cooking. Once cold, drizzle with olive oil and leave on the side to drain for 5 minutes. Give the pasta a good shake every minute or so.

2 Meanwhile cut the courgettes in half lengthways and then slice into 0.5cm half discs.

3 Heat 5 tablespoons of oil in a large frying pan over a medium heat and fry the courgettes for 5 minutes, stirring occasionally. Splash with the balsamic vinegar, add in the garlic and continue to cook for a further minute.

4 Scatter the mint over the courgettes, season with salt and pepper and mix all together. Set aside to cool.

5 Tip the pasta into a large bowl with the courgette mixture and feta cheese. Gently mix everything together to allow the flavours to combine. Leave to rest at room temperature for 5 minutes. Stir occasionally.

6 Once ready, serve immediately or keep in a sealed container in the fridge for the day after. Do not keep longer than 48 hours and always eat it at room temperature.

FARFALLE CON FAVE E PROSCIUTTO
Farfalle with broad beans and cooked ham

A traditional Roman recipe that never fails to impress. You can substitute the cooked ham with Parma ham or speck but never use buffalo mozzarella as it will release far too much milk and completely ruin the look of the dish. If you leave out the pasta it also makes a great side salad to accompany any meat.

Serves 4
500g farfalle
250g broad beans
8 tablespoons extra virgin olive oil, plus extra for drizzling
80g walnuts, roughly chopped
200g cooked ham, cut into 0.5cm cubes
200g cherry tomatoes, halved
2 mozzarella balls, drained and cut into small cubes
  (do not use buffalo mozzarella)
3 tablespoons freshly chopped flat leaf parsley
salt and pepper to taste

1 Pour 4 litres of water into a large saucepan and bring to the boil with 3 tablespoons of salt. Cook the pasta with the broad beans in the boiling salted water until al dente. Drain the pasta and beans through a colander and rinse under cold running water immediately, to stop the pasta cooking. Once cold, leave on the side to drain for 5 minutes. Drizzle with a little olive oil and give a good shake to the pasta every minute or so.

2 Meanwhile place the walnuts, ham, tomatoes, mozzarella and parsley in a large bowl. Pour over the extra virgin olive oil, season with salt and pepper and gently mix.

3 Add the pasta with the broad beans to the bowl and gently toss together to allow the flavours to combine.

4 Cover with cling film and leave to rest at room temperature for 15 minutes. Stir every 5 minutes.

5 Serve immediately or keep in a sealed container in the fridge for the day after. Do not keep longer than 48 hours and always eat it at room temperature.

RIGATONI AL PESTO ROSSO
Rigatoni with sun-dried tomato and basil pesto

If you are a fan of traditional tomato and basil sauce then you will love this recipe. The flavours are similar but the sun-dried tomatoes and Pecorino cheese are stronger in both smell and taste. People will feel that you are being extravagant when really the three ingredients are very similar to the basic Neapolitan sauce – this dish is just the posh version!

Serves 4
500g rigatoni
15 fresh basil leaves
250g sun-dried tomatoes in oil, reserve the oil
extra virgin olive oil, as required
50g freshly grated Pecorino cheese
salt and pepper to taste

1 Pour 4 litres of water in a large saucepan and bring to the boil with 2 tablespoons salt. Cook the pasta in the boiling salted water until al dente. Drain the pasta through a colander and rinse under cold running water immediately, to stop the pasta cooking. Once cold leave on the side to drain for 5 minutes. Give the pasta a good shake every minute or so.

2 Meanwhile place the basil and the sun-dried tomatoes with their reserved oil in a food processor. Blitz to create a smooth paste. If the paste is too dry add a little extra virgin olive oil to loosen it up.

3 Pour the tomato paste into a large bowl, fold in the Pecorino cheese and season with black pepper.

4 Tip the pasta into the bowl and gently mix everything together to allow the flavours to combine. Cover with cling film and leave to rest at room temperature for 15 minutes. Stir every 5 minutes.

5 Serve immediately or transfer to a sealed container and store in the fridge for the following day. Do not keep longer than 48 hours and always eat it at room temperature.

PASTA FOR THOSE WITH ALLERGIES

PAPPARDELLE ALLA BOSCAIOLA
Pappardelle with ham, mushrooms and cream
▶ EGG, FISH AND NUT FREE

In Naples where I come from, we don't often use cream in our pasta sauces, maybe because it's too hot or maybe instead because we tend to use cheese to get that creamy texture. When I arrived in England and found cream I loved experimenting with it. I wanted to create a fresh sauce, which the parsley, tomatoes and ham give you, but make it softer on the palate. I love this dish and it's so easy to make.

Serves 4
4 tablespoons olive oil
1 large white onion, finely sliced
250g cooked ham, diced
200g chestnut mushrooms, sliced
2 x 400g tins cherry tomatoes
100ml double cream
500g pappardelle
3 tablespoons freshly chopped flat leaf parsley
100g freshly grated Parmesan cheese
salt and pepper to taste

1 Heat the oil in a large frying pan or a wok over a medium heat and add the onion. Fry for about 5 minutes, stirring occasionally with a wooden spoon. Add in the ham and mushrooms and continue to cook for a further 3 minutes.

2 Pour in the cherry tomatoes and stir well. Simmer gently, uncovered, for 8 minutes, stirring every couple of minutes. Pour in the cream and season with salt and pepper. Mix everything together then remove from the heat and set aside.

3 Meanwhile cook the pasta in a large saucepan of boiling salted water until al dente. Drain and tip back into the same pan. Pour in the Boscaiola sauce with the parsley and stir everything together for 30 seconds to allow the flavours to combine.

4 Serve immediately with freshly grated Parmesan cheese sprinkled on top.

ZUPPA DI CIPOLLE E PASTINA
Onion and pancetta soup with pasta
► EGG, FISH AND NUT FREE

This recipe originally featured in my last book (*The Italian Diet*) as a soup dish. I had such amazing feedback that I have decided to turn it into a pasta soup. Believe you me, if you haven't tried this yet you are missing out – this is the ultimate comfort food.

Serves 4

150g pancetta or bacon rashers, rind removed
5 tablespoons extra virgin olive oil
700g white onions, peeled and finely sliced
1.8 litres chicken stock, made with 3 good-quality chicken stock cubes
1 x 400g tin chopped tomatoes
200g tiny pasta shells (look for conchigliette or lumachine)
6 fresh basil leaves, shredded
4 tablespoons freshly grated Pecorino or Parmesan cheese
salt and pepper to taste

1 Cut the pancetta or bacon into 0.5cm pieces and tip into a large saucepan. Place the saucepan over a medium heat and start to fry the pancetta for 2 minutes, stirring constantly.

2 Pour in the oil with the onions and stir everything together. Lower the heat and cook for 20 minutes, stirring occasionally, to allow the onions to take on a beautiful golden colour.

3 Once the onions are coloured, pour in the chicken stock and chopped tomatoes. Season to taste with salt and pepper and bring to the boil. Lower the heat, half cover the pan with a lid, and simmer for 20 minutes, stirring occasionally.

4 Add in the pasta and continue to cook, uncovered, over a low heat, for about 6 minutes or until the pasta is al dente. Stir every 2 minutes.

5 Once the pasta is cooked, remove the pan from the heat and stir in the basil and the cheese.

6 Serve immediately with some warm crusty bread.

PENNE CON SALSICCIA E RUCOLA
Penne with Italian sausages and rocket leaves
► GLUTEN, EGG, FISH AND NUT FREE

For everyone that is looking for a quick yet very tasty pasta dish, this is definitely the one to try. I absolutely love the combination of sausages, garlic and fennel seeds – it gives you the ultimate Italian flavours. If you can't find Italian sausages, try any good-quality ones, but please make sure that they have a very high meat content.

Serves 4

200g Italian sausages (check sausages are gluten free)
5 tablespoons extra virgin olive oil
1 garlic clove, peeled and thinly sliced
1 teaspoon fennel seeds
1/2 glass of dry white wine
500g gluten-free penne rigate
100g freshly grated Pecorino cheese
100g rocket leaves
salt to taste

1 Remove the skins from the sausages and place the meat mixture in a bowl.

2 Heat the oil in a large frying pan over a low heat and fry the sausage meat and the garlic for 3 minutes. Stir occasionally with a wooden spoon allowing the meat to crumble.

3 Add the fennel seeds, season with salt and continue to cook for 1 minute.

4 Pour in the wine and continue to cook for a further minute. Set aside away from the heat.

5 Meanwhile cook the pasta in a large saucepan of salted boiling water until al dente.

6 Once the pasta is cooked return the sauce over a medium heat. Drain the pasta and tip into the frying pan with the sauce.

7 Sprinkle over the Pecorino cheese and the rocket leaves and toss everything together over a medium heat for 30 seconds to allow the flavours to combine.

8 Serve immediately.

SPAGHETTI AL GORGONZOLA

Spaghetti with Gorgonzola and white wine sauce

▶ GLUTEN, EGG, FISH, MEAT AND NUT FREE

If you are watching your weight don't make this one! It tastes amazing and the butter, wine, cream and Gorgonzola make it worth eating, but I can't lie to you and try to give you healthy alternatives as this dish has to be left alone. Although you might think it's heavy – trust me, you will finish your portion and still want more. If it helps I can confirm that you will lose 105 calories for every 30 minutes of bedroom action, so enjoy both!

Serves 4
30g salted butter
200g Gorgonzola cheese, cut into chunks
150ml double cream
50ml dry white wine
2 tablespoons freshly chopped flat leaf parsley
½ teaspoon smoked paprika
500g gluten-free spaghetti
salt to taste

1 Melt the butter in a medium saucepan over a low heat. Add the Gorgonzola and cook for 2 minutes, stirring with a wooden spoon until melted.

2 Pour in the cream and wine and continue to cook for a further minute, stirring continuously, to allow the alcohol to evaporate.

3 Mix in the parsley and paprika, season with salt and set aside.

4 Cook the pasta in a large saucepan of boiling salted water until al dente. Drain and tip back into the same pan.

5 Pour in the Gorgonzola sauce and stir everything together for 30 seconds to allow the flavours to combine.

6 Serve immediately.

FUSILLI AL PESTO E YOGURT

Fusilli with basil pesto, lemon zest and yogurt

▶ EGG, MEAT AND FISH FREE

For anyone who is not very keen on basil pesto because it's too strong a flavour, this is a good alternative. By using Greek yogurt it makes the pesto smoother. Substitute the fusilli with farfalle if you prefer and please use a good-quality extra virgin olive oil.

Serves 4

60g fresh basil, leaves only
50g pine nuts
1 garlic clove, peeled
130ml extra virgin olive oil
zest of 1 unwaxed lemon
100g Greek-style yogurt
500g wholewheat fusilli
salt and pepper to taste

1 Place the basil, pine nuts and garlic in a food processor. Drizzle in the oil and blitz until smooth.

2 Transfer the basil mixture into a large bowl and fold in the lemon zest and yogurt. Season with salt and pepper and set aside.

3 Cook the pasta in a large saucepan of boiling salted water until al dente. Drain and tip into the bowl with the yogurt pesto. Toss everything together for 30 seconds to allow the pesto to coat the pasta evenly.

4 Serve immediately.

RIGATONI AL PECORINO SARDO
Rigatoni with soft cheese and Pecorino Sardo
► MEAT, FISH AND NUT FREE

In the summer of 2007 I spent a whole month on the island of Sardinia with my family. That is where my love affair with Pecorino Sardo cheese started. On the way back to London I bought so much of the cheese that I used it in all sorts of combinations but this is by far my favourite. A smooth plate of pasta with a great punchy flavour.

Serves 4
60g salted butter
250g soft cream cheese, e.g. Philadelphia
50ml full-fat milk
8 fresh basil leaves, finely chopped
100g freshly grated Pecorino Sardo
400g wholewheat rigatoni
salt and pepper to taste

1 Melt the butter in a medium saucepan over a low heat.

2 Tip in the cream cheese with the milk, basil and Pecorino cheese and cook for 1 minute, stirring continuously. Season with a little salt and plenty of black pepper. Remove from the heat and set aside.

3 Meanwhile cook the pasta in a large saucepan of boiling salted water until al dente. Drain and tip back into the same pan.

4 Pour in the cheese sauce and stir everything together for 30 seconds to allow the sauce to coat the pasta evenly.

5 Serve immediately.

CONCHIGLIETTE CON PISELLI, CAROTE E PANCETTA
Shell pasta with peas, carrots, pancetta and chilli
► GLUTEN, FISH AND NUT FREE

Is it soup? Is it pasta? It's both. A brilliant combination of a fresh vegetable broth but with the kick of pancetta and chilli. Adding the shell-shaped pasta finishes off this dish perfectly, making it extremely filling and tasty, yet it's still so easy to prepare – the ultimate one-pot dish. It can be eaten in smaller portions as a starter or as a main course.

Serves 4

5 tablespoons olive oil
1 large red onion, peeled and finely chopped
2 large carrots, peeled and diced about the size of a pea
250g pancetta, diced to the size of a pea
200g frozen peas, defrosted
1 teaspoon dried chilli flakes
1 litre vegetable stock, made with 2 good-quality
   vegetable stock cubes (check stock cubes are
   gluten free)
250g tiny shell gluten-free pasta
2 eggs
100g freshly grated Parmesan cheese
salt to taste

1 Heat the oil in a large saucepan over a medium heat and fry the onion and carrots for about 5 minutes until golden. Add the pancetta and continue to fry for a further 2 minutes. Stir occasionally with a wooden spoon.

2 Add in the peas and the chilli and continue to cook for 3 minutes, stirring occasionally.

3 Pour in the stock, lower the heat and leave to simmer for 15 minutes with the lid half on.

4 Remove the lid and add the pasta. Stir well and continue to cook over a low heat, uncovered, for about 8 minutes until the pasta start to soften. Stir every 2 minutes.

5 Once the pasta is al dente, remove the pan from the heat.

6 Crack in the eggs and mix for 30 seconds, allowing the broth to thicken.

7 Finally, add in the Parmesan cheese, check whether a little salt is needed and stir well. Serve immediately.

SPAGHETTI CON PESTO ALLA SICILIANA

Spaghetti with Sicilian pesto

▶ EGG, FISH AND MEAT FREE

This is a recipe that you will find in every cookery book in Italy but mine will guarantee maximum satisfaction. Never use dried sun-dried tomatoes because they will be too salty but you can substitute the almonds with pine nuts if you prefer. Honestly for this dish you can really use any shape of pasta you wish – enjoy!

Serves 4

50g skinned almonds
20 medium fresh basil leaves, plus extra to serve
150g sun-dried tomatoes in oil, drained
4 garlic cloves, peeled and halved
extra virgin olive oil, as required
80g freshly grated Parmesan cheese
500g wholewheat spaghetti
salt and pepper to taste

1 Place the almonds in a frying pan over a medium heat and toast until golden brown all over. Set aside to cool.

2 Place the basil and sun-dried tomatoes in a food processor with the garlic. As you start to blitz, pour in enough oil to create a smooth paste.

3 Add the almonds and continue to blitz until creamy. Add more oil if necessary.

4 Transfer the mixture to a large bowl and use a fork to fold in the Parmesan cheese. Season with salt and pepper and set aside.

5 Cook the pasta in a large saucepan with plenty of boiling salted water until al dente. Drain well and tip into the bowl with the pesto. Mix everything together for 30 seconds to allow the pesto to coat the spaghetti.

6 Serve immediately, with a few basil leaves scattered on top.

DITALINI ALLA CREMA VERDE
Ditalini with spinach and Parmesan cheese

▶ EGG, FISH, MEAT AND NUT FREE

For anyone who loves spinach, this is the dish for you. As you can see from the ingredients there are very few things to buy and yet the flavour is amazing. I have tried this recipe with rocket instead of spinach and it works just as well. Please make sure you use fresh rather than frozen spinach.

Serves 4
20g salted butter
1 onion, peeled and finely chopped
200g fresh spinach leaves, washed
100ml hot vegetable stock
350g ditalini
60g freshly grated Parmesan cheese
salt and pepper to taste

1 Melt the butter in a medium saucepan over a low heat and fry the onion for about 3 minutes, stirring with a wooden spoon until golden.

2 Add the spinach with the stock and cook, uncovered, over a medium heat for 10 minutes, stirring every 2–3 minutes.

3 Meanwhile cook the pasta in a large saucepan of boiling salted water for 2 minutes less than the packet instructions. Drain and tip into the saucepan with the spinach. Continue to cook the pasta for a further 2 minutes with the spinach to allow the flavours to combine. Season with salt and pepper and stir occasionally.

4 Serve hot, topped with plenty of grated Parmesan cheese.

LINGUINE CON CIPOLLE E ACCIUGHE
Linguine with sautéed red onions and anchovies
▶ GLUTEN, EGG, MEAT AND NUT FREE

If you love anchovies and you fancy something full of flavour this is a really exciting dish to try. It's colourful and extremely easy to prepare. Use anchovies preserved in oil rather than those marinated in vinegar. If you prefer you can substitute the linguine with spaghetti.

Serves 4

80g salted butter
500g red onions, peeled and finely sliced
150ml warm water
100g anchovies in oil, drained and chopped
3 tablespoons freshly chopped flat leaf parsley
500g gluten-free linguine
salt and pepper to taste

1 Melt the butter in a medium saucepan over a medium heat and fry the onions for 5 minutes, stirring occasionally with a wooden spoon.

2 Pour in the warm water and continue to cook for a further 40 minutes, stirring every 5 minutes.

3 Stir in the anchovies and continue to cook for 5 minutes until the anchovies are completely dissolved. Sprinkle over the parsley and set aside, away from the heat.

4 Meanwhile cook the pasta in a large saucepan of boiling salted water until al dente. Drain and tip back into the same pan.

5 Pour in the onion and anchovy sauce and stir everything together over a low heat for 30 seconds to allow the flavours to combine. Season to taste with a little salt and pepper.

6 Serve immediately.

FUSILLI ALLA PIZZAIOLA ▸ GLUTEN, EGG, DAIRY, FISH, MEAT AND NUT FREE
Fusilli with garlic, chopped tomatoes and oregano

I like this recipe because you can also use the sauce to accompany grilled chicken or fish. This pasta will take you a little over ten minutes to prepare and will make you feel really satisfied.

Serves 4
6 tablespoons extra virgin olive oil
3 garlic cloves, peeled and finely sliced
2 x 400g tins chopped tomatoes
10 pitted Kalamata olives, halved
2 teaspoons dried oregano (or fresh if you have some)
500g gluten-free fusilli
salt and pepper to taste

1 Heat the oil in a large frying pan over a medium heat and fry the garlic for about 1 minute, stirring with a wooden spoon.

2 Pour in the chopped tomatoes with the olives and oregano. Stir and gently simmer, uncovered, for 10 minutes, stirring every couple of minutes.

3 Once ready, season with salt and pepper, remove from the heat and set aside.

4 Meanwhile cook the pasta in a large saucepan of boiling salted water until al dente. Drain and tip back into the same pan.

5 Return the pan to a low heat, pour in the Pizzaiola sauce and stir everything together for 30 seconds to allow the flavours to combine.

6 Serve immediately – without any kind of cheese on top.

PASTA E ZUCCA ▶ MEAT, FISH AND NUT FREE
Pasta soup with pumpkin, eggs and Cheddar cheese

A typical winter soup in the D'Acampo family, always eaten one or two days after Halloween. There are so many carved pumpkins around our house that I had to come up with a recipe to try and eat some of them!

Serves 4

4 tablespoons olive oil

1 large white onion, peeled and finely chopped

300g prepared pumpkin flesh (without skin or seeds), cut into 1cm cubes

2 litres hot vegetable stock, made with 3 good-quality vegetable stock cubes

250g medium shell pasta (look for conchiglie)

3 eggs

50g grated Cheddar cheese

3 tablespoons freshly chopped flat leaf parsley

salt and pepper to taste

1 Heat the oil in a large saucepan over a medium heat and fry the onion for about 5 minutes until golden. Add in the pumpkin and continue to fry for a further 2 minutes. Stir occasionally with a wooden spoon.

2 Pour in the stock, lower the heat and leave to simmer for 15 minutes with the lid half on.

3 Remove the lid and season with salt and pepper. Add in the pasta and continue to cook, uncovered, over a low heat, for about 6 minutes. Stir every 2 minutes.

4 Once the pasta is cooked, remove the pan from the heat. Crack in the eggs and mix everything together for 30 seconds to allow the broth to thicken.

5 Stir in the Cheddar cheese and serve immediately, sprinkled with parsley.

pasta for those with allergies **197**

PENNE AL MASCARPONE E PANCETTA
Penne with mascarpone, pancetta and Parmesan
▶ GLUTEN, EGG, FISH AND NUT FREE

Aubergines are an amazing vegetable that often get forgotten. The flavours of the pancetta, Parmesan cheese, parsley and aubergine are fabulous on their own, but adding in the mascarpone gives the perfect creamy texture without any heaviness. You can substitute the Parmesan for Pecorino cheese and the pancetta for bacon if you prefer.

Serves 4
2 tablespoons olive oil
1 tablespoon salted butter
250g cubed pancetta
1 medium aubergine, trimmed and cut into 1cm cubes
250g mascarpone cheese
500g gluten-free penne rigate
4 tablespoons finely chopped flat leaf parsley
4 tablespoons freshly grated Parmesan cheese
salt and pepper to taste

1 Heat the oil and butter in a large frying pan or a wok over a medium heat and add the pancetta and aubergine. Fry for about 5 minutes until golden and crispy, stirring occasionally with a wooden spoon.

2 Tip in the mascarpone cheese, stir everything to combine and continue to cook for a further 2 minutes. Season with salt and pepper. Remove from the heat and set aside.

3 Cook the pasta in a large saucepan of boiling salted water until al dente. Drain and tip back into the same pan, off the heat. Stir in the mascarpone sauce with the parsley and the Parmesan cheese.

4 Mix everything together for 30 seconds to allow the sauce to coat the pasta evenly.

5 Serve immediately.

ZUPPA DI PASTA CON PATATE E PORRI
Pasta soup with potatoes, pancetta and leeks
▶ EGG, FISH AND NUT FREE

Many people would never associate pasta and potato but in this case you are really going to have to trust me. This recipe has been in my family for over fifty years and considering that so far there have been two chefs in the family, it must be *fantastico*! Make sure you use a floury potato like a Maris Piper and you can substitute pancetta with bacon if you wish.

Serves 4
6 tablespoons olive oil
1 large leek, washed and finely chopped
250g pancetta, cubed
1 large carrot, peeled and cut into 0.5cm cubes
400g floury potatoes, peeled and cut into 1cm cubes
1.8 litres hot vegetable stock, made with 3 good-quality
  vegetable stock cubes
1 x 400g tin chopped tomatoes, use 3 tablespoons only
250g farfalline
60g freshly grated Parmesan cheese
salt and pepper to taste

1 Heat the olive oil in a large saucepan over a medium heat and fry the leek and pancetta for about 3 minutes. Add in the carrot and potato and continue to fry for a further 2 minutes. Stir occasionally with a wooden spoon.

2 Pour in the stock, lower the heat and leave to simmer, uncovered, for 20 minutes.

3 Mix in 3 tablespoons chopped tomatoes and season with salt and pepper.

4 Add in the pasta and continue to cook, uncovered, over a low heat, for about 6 minutes or until the pasta is al dente. Stir every 2 minutes.

5 Once the pasta is cooked, remove the pan from the heat and stir in the Parmesan cheese.

6 Serve immediately with some warm crusty bread.

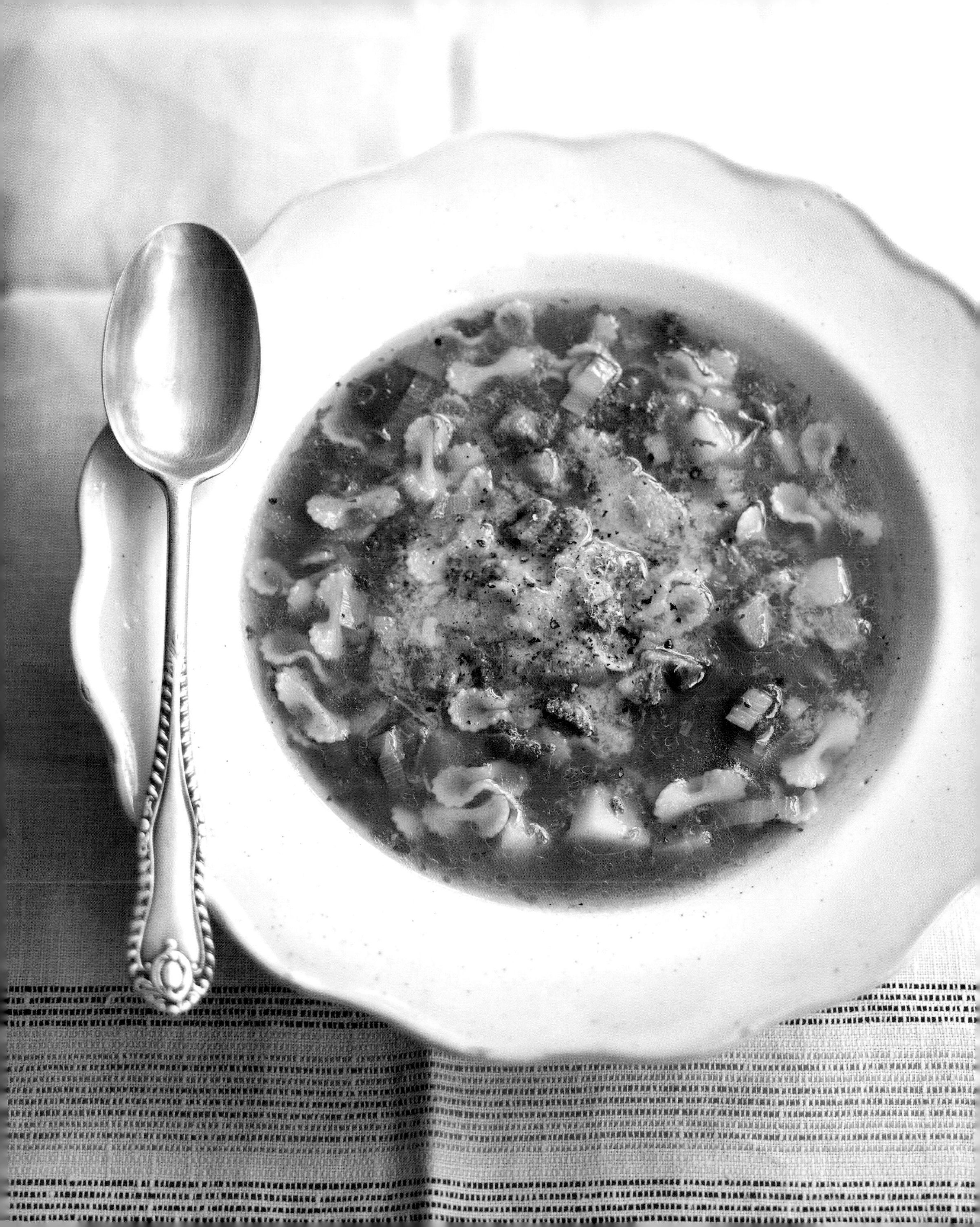

PASTA E CAVOLFIORE

Shell pasta with cauliflower, eggs and Parmesan cheese

▶ GLUTEN, FISH AND NUT FREE

When I first described this dish to my family, they thought I was mad. They couldn't understand how the combination of flavours would taste nice and I'm happy to say that now they admit defeat. They loved it and now I have to make it at least a couple of times a month, even more in the winter. It is such a homely dish and couldn't be easier to prepare, yet will leave you completely satisfied. Try it and see!

Serves 4

5 tablespoons olive oil
1 large white onion, peeled and finely chopped
250g cauliflower florets, roughly chopped
1.8 litres hot chicken stock, made with 3 good-quality chicken stock cubes
300g medium gluten-free shell pasta (look for conchiglie)
3 eggs
100g freshly grated Parmesan cheese
salt and pepper to taste

1 Heat the oil in a large saucepan over a medium heat and fry the onion for 3–5 minutes until golden. Add in the cauliflower and continue to fry for a further 2 minutes, stirring occasionally with a wooden spoon.

2 Pour in the stock, lower the heat and leave to simmer for 15 minutes with the lid half on.

3 Remove the lid, season with salt and pepper and add the pasta. Continue to cook, uncovered, over a low heat, for about 8 minutes until the pasta is al dente, stirring every 2 minutes.

4 Remove the pan from the heat, crack in the eggs and mix everything together for 30 seconds to thicken the broth.

5 Finally, add in the Parmesan cheese, stir and serve immediately.

PENNE IN SALSA ROSA
Penne served in a pink tomato and cream sauce

▶ GLUTEN, EGG, FISH, MEAT AND NUT FREE

This recipe reminds me of my boys as it was their first real pasta dish. The cream makes the tomato and basil sauce much milder on the palate and of course it will be a big hit with little girls as the sauce is pink. It is a really easy dish to make and is perfect for a small child being introduced to new flavours. Substitute the penne with spaghetti if you prefer.

Serves 4

6 tablespoons extra virgin olive oil
1 onion, finely chopped
700ml passata (sieved tomatoes)
10 fresh basil leaves
100ml double cream
500g gluten-free penne rigate
salt and white pepper to taste

1 Heat the oil in a medium saucepan over a low heat and fry the onion for 3–5 minutes until golden, stirring with a wooden spoon.

2 Pour in the passata, add the basil leaves and season with salt and pepper. Cook, uncovered, over a medium heat for 10 minutes, stirring every 2–3 minutes.

3 Pour in the cream and continue to cook for a further 5 minutes.

4 Meanwhile cook the pasta in a large saucepan of boiling salted water until al dente. Drain and tip back into the same pan. Pour in the tomato and cream sauce and stir everything together for 30 seconds to allow the flavours to combine.

5 Serve immediately.

INDEX

al dente 10, 14–15

anchovies:
- spaghetti with breadcrumbs, garlic and 76
- linguine with cherry tomatoes, capers and 118–19
- linguine with sautéed red onions and 194

asparagus sauce, rigatoni with 79

beef:
- baked pasta with meat sauce and Parmesan cheese 100–1
- fettuccine with meat and red wine sauce 26–7
- lasagne with pesto 121

borlotti beans, spicy pasta with cannellini beans and 129

broad beans, farfalle with cooked ham and 174

broccoli, pasta shells with chilli, pine nuts and 53

bucatini with eggs, pancetta and Pecorino Romano 147

cake, sweet pasta 109

candied fruit, half-moon shaped sweet pasta filled with 106–7

cannellini beans, spicy pasta with borlotti beans and 129

cannelloni:
- with rocket, spinach and ricotta cheese 84
- with sun-dried tomatoes, mozzarella and basil 93
- with tuna, ricotta cheese and lemon 98

carbohydrates 8–10

cheese:
- baked pasta with ham and 90
- baked pasta with meat sauce and Parmesan cheese 100–1
- cannelloni filled with sun-dried tomatoes, mozzarella and basil 93
- filled pasta with roasted butternut squash 24
- fresh pasta with chicken and Dolcelatte 30
- fusilli with four cheeses and chives 135
- pasta salad with walnuts and Gorgonzola cheese 156
- pasta soup with pumpkin, eggs and Cheddar cheese 197

penne with feta cheese, cherry tomatoes and mint 166

penne with mascarpone, pancetta and Parmesan 199

rigatoni with soft cheese and Pecorino Sardo 187

shell pasta with tomato, mozzarella and fresh basil 168–9

spaghetti with Gorgonzola and white wine sauce 184

see also ricotta cheese

chicken, fresh pasta with Dolcelatte and 30

chicory, penne with sausages, red wine and 63

chillies:
- penne with red chillies, garlic and chopped tomatoes 122
- spaghetti with garlic, olive oil and 130
- spicy chorizo and ricotta stuffed ravioli 45

chocolate chips, half-moon shaped pasta filled with hazelnuts and 110

chorizo and ricotta stuffed ravioli 45

courgettes:
- crispy topped pasta with salami and 96
- fusilli with red peppers and 56
- gnocchetti with courgettes in butter and sage sauce 114
- pasta salad with balsamic vinegar and 172
- penne with smoked salmon, lemon zest and 161
- shell pasta with courgettes, garlic and pancetta sauce 155
- spicy tagliatelle with peppers, red onions, thyme and 33

crab, pasta with fresh chilli, lemon zest and 116

ditalini with spinach and Parmesan cheese 193

eggs:
- bucatini with pancetta, Pecorino Romano and 147
- egg pasta dough 19
- pasta bake with pancetta, rosemary and minced pork 158
- pasta soup with pumpkin, Cheddar cheese and 197
- shell pasta with cauliflower, Parmesan and 202

spaghetti frittata with Parmesan and rocket 154

farfalle:
- crispy topped farfalle with smoked salmon and chives 87
- pasta baked with peppers and mozzarella 103
- pasta salad with walnuts and Gorgonzola cheese 156
- with broad beans and cooked ham 174

farfalline:
- pasta soup with potatoes, pancetta and leeks 200
- three bean and tuna pasta salad 164

fettuccine:
- baked pasta with meat sauce and Parmesan cheese 100–1
- with chicken and Dolcelatte 30
- with meat and red wine sauce 26–7
- with sweet onions, rosemary and minced lamb 37

fusilli:
- pasta salad with courgettes and balsamic vinegar 172
- with basil pesto, lemon zest and yogurt 186
- with black olive tapenade 160
- with chestnut mushrooms, leeks and mascarpone cheese 66
- with four cheeses and chives 135
- with garlic, chopped tomatoes and oregano 196
- with prawns and basil pesto 151
- with red peppers and courgettes 56

glycaemic index (GI) 9–11

gluten-free pasta 13, 183, 184, 188, 194, 196, 199, 202, 205

gnocchetti: with courgettes in butter and sage sauce 114

gnocchi:
- potato dumplings with tomato sauce and Cheddar cheese 88
- with Parma ham 104

green beans, pasta shells with cherry tomatoes and 153

green pasta 19

half-moon shaped pasta:
- with candied fruit 106–7
- with chocolate chips and hazelnuts

110
with ham and sun-dried tomatoes 38
ham:
    baked pasta with cheeses and 90
    fresh tagliatelle with artichokes and
        Parma ham 48
    half-moon shaped pasta filled with
        sun-dried tomatoes and 38
    linguine served with a delicate
        saffron sauce 75
    farfalle with broad beans and cooked
        ham 174
    pappardelle with mushrooms, cream
        and 178
    semolina gnocchi with Parma ham
        104

lamb, pasta with sweet onions, rosemary
    and 37
lasagne with pesto 121
linguine:
    seafood pasta with chilli and white
        wine 65
    with cherry tomatoes, anchovies and
        capers 118–19
    with cherry tomatoes, pancetta and
        white wine 143
    with crab, fresh chilli and lemon zest
        116
    with a delicate saffron sauce 75
    with Genovese basil pesto 62
    with mussels, garlic and white wine
        131
    with sautéed red onions and
        anchovies 194
    with smoked salmon and spicy red
        pepper sauce 72
    with tinned tuna, olives and chilli 54
lobster, spaghettini with white wine and
    60

minerals 11, 12
mushrooms:
    fusilli with chestnut mushrooms,
        leeks and mascarpone cheese 66
    pappardelle with ham, cream
        and 178
    penne with sausages, rosemary
        and porcini mushrooms 46
    saffron pappardelle with Marsala
        and 44

Northern Italian salad 125
nutrition 8–13

onions:
    onion and pancetta soup 180

tagliatelle in creamy tartare sauce
    34
fettuccine with sweet onions,
    rosemary and minced lamb 37
linguine with sautéed red onions
    and anchovies 194

pancetta:
    bucatini with eggs, Pecorino
        Romano and 147
    linguine with cherry tomatoes, white
        wine and 143
    onion and pancetta soup 180
    pasta bake with rosemary, minced
        pork and 158
    pasta soup with potatoes, leeks and
        200
    penne with mascarpone, Parmesan
        and 199
    shell pasta with courgettes, garlic
        and pancetta sauce 155
    shell pasta with peas, carrots, chilli
        and 188
    spicy pasta with borlotti and
        cannellini beans 129
pappardelle:
    saffron pappardelle 22
    saffron pappardelle with Marsala
        and mushrooms 44
    with ham, mushrooms and cream
        178
pasta shells:
    and beans with squid and chorizo 70
    spicy pasta with borlotti and
        cannellini beans 129
    with cauliflower, eggs and Parmesan
        202
    with courgettes, garlic and
        pancetta sauce 155
    with green beans and cherry
        tomatoes 153
    with peas, carrots, pancetta and
        chilli 188
    with pork and rosemary 94
    with prawns and saffron 89
    with spicy pork and tomato sauce
        138
    with sprouting broccoli, chilli and
        pine nuts 53
    with tomato, mozzarella and fresh
        basil 168–9
penne:
    baked pasta with ham and
        cheeses 90
    crispy topped pasta with courgettes
        and salami 96
    pasta bake with pancetta,

rosemary and minced pork 158
in a pink tomato and cream sauce
    205
with cherry tomatoes, garlic, olives
    and capers 171
with red chicory, sausages and red
    wine 63
with courgettes, smoked salmon and
    lemon zest 161
with feta cheese, cherry tomatoes
    and mint 166
with Italian sausages and rocket 183
with mascarpone, pancetta and
    Parmesan 199
with peas, pork, rosemary and white
    wine 74
with red chillies, garlic and chopped
    tomatoes 122
with roasted peppers and mozzarella
    105
peppers:
    fusilli with red peppers and
        courgettes 56
    linguine with smoked salmon and
        spicy red pepper sauce 72
    Northern Italian salad with roasted
        peppers 125
    pasta baked with mozzarella
        and 103
    penne with roasted peppers and
        mozzarella 105
    spaghetti with yellow peppers, chilli
        and herbs 81
    spicy tagliatelle with courgettes, red
        onions, thyme and 33
pesto:
    fusilli with basil pesto, lemon zest
        and yogurt 186
    lasagne with pesto 121
    linguine with Genovese basil pesto
        62
    fusilli with prawns and basil pesto
        151
    spaghetti with Sicilian pesto 191
    spaghettini with scallops and parsley
        pesto 69
pork:
    baked pasta with meat sauce and
        Parmesan cheese 100–1
    fettuccine with meat and red wine
        sauce 26–7
    pasta bake with pancetta,
        rosemary and minced pork 158
    penne with peas, rosemary, white
        wine and 74
    shell pasta with rosemary and 94
    shell pasta with spicy pork and

tomato sauce 138
potatoes, pasta soup with pancetta, leeks and 200
prawns:
    tagliatelle with a creamy brandy sauce and 29
    fusilli with basil pesto and 151
    shell pasta with saffron and 89
pumpkin, pasta soup with eggs, Cheddar cheese and 197

ragù sauce 26–7
ravioli:
    spicy chorizo and ricotta stuffed 45
    with smoked salmon and lemon zest 42–3
ricotta cheese:
    cannelloni filled with sun-dried tomatoes, mozzarella and basil 93
    cannelloni filled with tuna, lemon and 98
    half-moon shaped pasta filled with chocolate chips and hazelnuts 110
    half-moon shaped pasta filled with ham and sun-dried tomatoes 38
    half-moon shaped sweet pasta filled with candied fruit 106–7
    spaghetti with toasted pine nuts and 126
    spicy chorizo and ricotta stuffed ravioli 45
rigatoni:
    with artichokes, garlic and orange zest 59
    with aubergines, garlic and cherry tomatoes 163
    with creamy asparagus sauce, peas and porcini mushrooms 79
    with soft cheese and Pecorino Sardo 187
    with sun-dried tomato paste and basil 175

salads:
    Northern Italian salad with roasted peppers 125
    three bean and tuna pasta salad 164
    with courgettes and balsamic vinegar 172
    with walnuts and Gorgonzola cheese 156
salami, crispy topped pasta with courgettes and 96
sausages:
    penne with Italian sausages and rocket 183
    tagliatelle with rosemary, porcini

mushrooms and 46
    penne with red chicory, red wine and 63
scallops, spaghettini with parsley pesto and 69
seafood pasta with chilli and white wine 65
semolina gnocchi with Parma ham 104
smoked salmon:
    crispy topped farfalle with 87
    linguine with spicy red pepper sauce and 72
    penne with courgettes, lemon zest and 161
    ravioli with lemon zest and 42–3
soups:
    chunky vegetable and pasta soup 132
    onion and pancetta soup with pasta 180
    pasta soup with potatoes, pancetta and leeks 200
    pasta soup with pumpkin, eggs and Cheddar cheese 197
spaghetti:
    and spinach tart 99
    spaghetti frittata with Parmesan and rocket 154
    with anchovies, breadcrumbs and garlic 76
    with basil and tomato sauce 137
    with clams, garlic and chilli 140
    with garlic, olive oil and chilli 130
    with Gorgonzola and white wine sauce 184
    with ricotta cheese and toasted pine nuts 126
    with Sicilian pesto 191
    with yellow peppers, chilli and herbs 81
spaghettini:
    with lobster and white wine 60
    with scallops and parsley pesto 69
spinach:
    cannelloni filled with rocket, ricotta cheese and 84
    ditalini with Parmesan cheese and 193
    green pasta 19
    spaghetti and spinach tart 99
sweet pasta cake 109

tagliatelle 21
    in creamy tartare sauce 34
    with artichokes and Parma ham 48
    with butter and truffle shavings 41
    with peppers, courgettes, red onions

and thyme 33
    with prawns and a creamy brandy sauce 29
    with sausages, rosemary and porcini mushrooms 46
tart, spaghetti and spinach 99
tomatoes:
    cannelloni filled with sun-dried tomatoes, mozzarella and basil 93
    fusilli with garlic, chopped tomatoes and oregano 196
    lasagne with pesto 121
    linguine with cherry tomatoes, anchovies and capers 118–19
    pasta shells with green beans and cherry tomatoes 153
    penne served in a pink tomato and cream sauce 205
    penne with cherry tomatoes, pancetta and white wine 143
    pappardelle with ham, mushrooms and cream 178
    penne with red chillies, garlic and chopped tomatoes 122
    penne with cherry tomatoes, garlic, olives and capers 171
    penne with feta cheese, cherry tomatoes and mint 166
    potato dumplings with tomato sauce and Cheddar cheese 88
    rigatoni with aubergines, garlic and cherry tomatoes 163
    rigatoni with sun-dried tomato paste and basil 175
    seafood pasta with chilli and white wine 65
    shell pasta with mozzarella, fresh basil and 168–9
    shell pasta with spicy pork and tomato sauce 138
    spaghetti with basil and tomato sauce 137
    tomato pasta 19
truffle shavings, fresh tagliatelle served with butter and 41
tuna:
    cannelloni filled with ricotta cheese, lemon and 98
    linguine with olives, chilli and 54
    three bean and tuna pasta salad 164

vermicelli: sweet pasta cake 109
vitamins 11, 12

wholewheat pasta 11–12, 186, 187, 191